P9-AGP-548

DATE DUE

NO 25 98		
DE 16 98		
MY 31 '01		
NO 15 01		
MR 26 '03		

DEMCO 38-296

REDUCING
FIREARM INJURY
AND DEATH

REDUCING FIREARM INJURY AND DEATH

A Public Health Sourcebook on Guns

Trudy Ann Karlson, Ph.D.

&

Stephen W. Hargarten, M.D., M.P.H.

RUTGERS UNIVERSITY PRESS *New Brunswick, New Jersey and London*

Riverside Community College
Library
4800 Magnolia Avenue
Riverside, CA 92506

RA 772 .F57 K37 1997

Karlson, Trudy Ann.

Reducing firearm injury and
death

Copyright © 1997 by Trudy Ann Karlson and Stephen W. Hargarten
All rights reserved. No part of this book may be reproduced or utilized in any form or by
any means, electronic or mechanical, or by any information storage and retrieval system,
without written permission from the publisher. Please contact Rutgers University Press,
Livingston Campus, Bldg. 4161, P.O. Box 5062, New Brunswick, New Jersey 08903. The
only exception to this prohibition is "fair use" as defined by U.S. copyright law.

Library of Congress Cataloging-in-Publication Data

Karlson, Trudy Ann.
Reducing firearm injury and death : a public health sourcebook on guns / Trudy Ann
Karlson, Stephen W. Hargarten.
    p.   cm.
Includes bibliographical references and index.
ISBN 0-8135-2420-2 (cloth : alk. paper). — ISBN 0-8135-2421-0 (pbk. : alk. paper)
1. Firearms accidents—Prevention.   2. Firearms—Design and construction.
3. Firearms—Marketing. I. Hargarten, Stephen W.   II. Title.
RA772.F57K37 1997
363.3'3—dc21
                                                                        97-1803
                                                                          CIP
British Cataloging-in-Publication information available.

Manufactured in the United States of America
DESIGN, COMPOSITION, AND COPY EDITING BY ELIZABETH M. BURKE

CONTENTS

FIGURES

TABLES

FOREWORD

Guns don't spontaneously generate. People manufacture them. And when they do, they manufacture the gun pursuant to a design, and they market the gun according to a plan. The designs and plans are chosen to maximize the revenue of the corporation making the gun. Nothing unusual about this; the same could be said for most, if not all products. But with these other products, there are parameters within which design and marketing decisions can be made. The parameters are set by regulation. Not so with guns.

Guns occupy a special place in American society. They have a talismanic quality that has protected them from interference by government regulation. Or, more precisely, groups of people have organized themselves around the mission of protecting guns from regulation. For these people, the gun seems to be the physical representation of the twin virtues of freedom and self-protection. Take away the gun, they argue, and you have laid yourself bare to tyranny and victimization.

There is another argument, however, that looks at the almost forty thousand gun-related deaths per year in the United States and finds that the toll of guns, particularly handguns, has become unacceptable. Gunfire is the leading cause of death for some groups of the population, and therefore the vehicle of these deaths—the gun—must come under control.

Not only is agreement between the two sides to this debate absent, but so is meaningful communication. Someone who fervently believes that handguns are needed for protection and the preservation of freedom is not prone to realize that guns are, on balance, detrimental to the public's health. Individuals understandably tend to measure risk on an individual rather than a population basis. But the fields of public health and public policy are dependent upon risk/benefit ratios at the community level. Society frequently asks individuals to compromise their personal interests for the common good. Immunizations, with their small risk of adverse reactions, are a clear example of this. We legally require individuals to assume a limited risk for the benefit of us all. Most individuals accept this type of risk in order to enhance the common good.

But there is a very vocal segment of the American population that refuses to consider any option other than having the unfettered freedom to possess any weapon of their choice. Perhaps the fear of tyranny and victimization is so great, and the love of freedom so strong, that arguments regarding the benefits of regulating guns go unrecognized by them. But the benefits are real. They present themselves as reductions in domestic abuse, teenage suicide, drive-by shootings, and the fear of some citizens to walk the streets past dusk. Attainment of these benefits may call for some compromises by those who view the gun as their insurance policy for freedom and safety.

What types of compromises might be possible? One answer to this question returns us directly to design and marketing issues. The key to reducing the incidence of gun deaths need not be the public health police's midnight knock on the door to confiscate the family gun. The key may be in the redesign of the gun and the regulation of its marketing.

Personalized handguns, or handguns that will only operate for an authorized user, have the potential for reducing unintended shootings by children, teenage suicides, and even some homicidal shootings. The technology for personalized handguns is clearly within our grasp. Regulation of the way handguns are marketed—for example, disallowing advertisements that appeal to criminal misuse of guns—are both reasonable and feasible.

Achievement of design and marketing regulation of handguns, however, will require a reorientation of public policy. To date, our country's policies have focused more on the person pulling the trigger than the person making the trigger. The public health orientation to reducing handgun deaths includes a focus on the product involved in the injuries, as well as the persons involved.

This book, written by two experts trained in public health and injury prevention, provides the foundation for approaching gun injuries as a public health problem. In its chapters, the authors provide details on gun deaths, wound ballistics, the gun industry, gun policy, and perhaps most importantly, the gun itself. An understanding of the anatomy and functioning of handguns will be of considerable benefit to those trying to formulate product-related strategies for the reduction of gun injuries.

Within the next decade, the design of handguns could be modified not to increase their lethality, as has been the trend in recent times, but to reduce the likelihood of certain types of gun deaths. This primer will serve as an effective tool in the achievement of that goal.

Stephen P. Teret, J.D., M.P.H.
Professor and Director
The Johns Hopkins Center for Gun Policy and Research
July 1996

Foreword

ACKNOWLEDGMENTS

The authors gratefully acknowledge the help of many, without whom this work would not have been possible. First, we would like to thank the Joyce Foundation, which provided funds for a significant portion of the writing. Their support of activities that are geared toward reducing gun-related deaths and injuries is rare and unusual in the world of philanthropy.

Our reviewers generously made helpful suggestions—correcting our technical errors, calling attention to new information and concepts, and giving us support in other ways as well. Our reviewers are not, however, responsible for any remaining technical errors nor for the views the authors have expressed regarding the public health implications of this information. Reviewers were:

KRIS BOSWORTH, PH.D., Director, Center for Adolescent Studies, School of Education, Indiana University, Bloomington, Indiana

SUSAN GALLAGHER, M.P.H., Director, and ANARA GUARD, M.L.S., Information Specialist, Children's Safety Network, Education Development Center, Newton, Massachusetts

MONTY LUTZ, Forensic Scientist, State of Wisconsin Crime Laboratory, Wisconsin Department of Justice, Milwaukee, Wisconsin

JAMES MERCY, PH.D., Division of Violence Prevention, National Center for Injury Prevention and Control, Centers for Disease Control, Atlanta, Georgia

ED QUEBBEMAN, M.D., PH.D., Professor, Department of Surgery, Medical College of Wisconsin, Milwaukee, Wisconsin

JON VERNICK, J.D., M.P.H., Associate Director, Center for Gun Policy and Research, The Johns Hopkins School of Hygiene and Public Health, Baltimore, Maryland

We would also like to acknowledge the pioneering work of our teachers, the late William Haddon, Jr., M.D., former president, Insurance Institute for Highway Safety, and Professor Susan Baker, The Johns Hopkins School of Hygiene and Public Health. Dr. Haddon and Professor Baker not only taught us the science of injury control, but through their commitment to reducing unnecessary death

xii   and disabilities from injuries, encouraged us to pursue the special blend of science, policy research, and civic action necessary to accomplish our goals.

We are fortunate to count as colleagues Stephen Teret, J.D., M.P.H., Director, Center for Gun Policy and Research, The Johns Hopkins School of Hygiene and Public Health; Garen Wintemute, M.D., M.P.H., Director, Violence Prevention Research Program, at University of California Davis; and Arthur Kellermann, M.D., M.P.H., Director, Center for Injury Control, Emory University School of Public Health. Each of them has made ground-breaking contributions to the reduction of firearm injuries. We have made ample use of their work in this text.

Several others gave us valued assistance in research, writing, and illustrations. We thank our colleagues Chip Quade, for his research, writing, and organizational help; Patricia Beutel, Mallory O'Brien, Traci Tymus, and Beth George for their assistance in finding current data; and Mary Ann Sveum for her manuscript preparation. We also thank Lynn Entine for her editing and organization, Susan Kummer and Ann Stretton of Artifax for illustrations, and Robert Drea for his photography. The State of Wisconsin Crime Laboratory made available several exhibits for use as illustrations.

Finally, we would like to acknowledge the support of our spouses, David Weber and Janis Cohn, and our children, Andy and Will Karlson-Weber, Beth Hering, and Jordan and Leah Hargarten. As always, our hope is for a safer world for them to live in.

Acknowledgments

INTRODUCTION: *Why We Are Writing This Book*

Reducing Firearm Injury and Death began when we first started doing research on firearms. As an injury epidemiologist (Trudy Karlson), and an emergency medicine physician (Stephen Hargarten), we know deaths from firearms are more common than deaths from motor vehicle crashes in some communities in the United States. We know that those who survive shootings are often permanently disabled and require expensive care. From our past experience in studying how to reduce deaths and injuries from motor vehicles and other causes, we felt certain that with appropriate product design strategies based on sound scientific knowledge, deaths and injuries from firearms could also be reduced.

We soon learned, however, that we didn't know much about guns themselves or how guns cause injury. Then we discovered that the information we wanted was not easy to come by. Available popular literature on guns either focused on hunting or otherwise assumed readers had a working knowledge of guns. Popular literature also was often filled with polemic and espoused views that that made us wonder whether the information was sound. Information in the academic literature, while growing in recent years, was scattered among journals in fields as diverse as criminology and health services research. Texts on guns and gunshot wounds were few, and those available were written for medical examiners or those interested in military ballistics. So, in many ways, this is the book we wished we had had when we were starting out—a primer on how guns work, how they cause injury, and on strategies based on the public health perspective for change.

Approaches to Firearm Injuries and Deaths

We are public health professionals trained in injury control. This means our approach is different from the strategies commonly chosen to address gun-related deaths and injuries in this country: approaches based on criminal justice, mental health, safety education, and violence prevention. We briefly summarize these strategies here and explain how our public health approach differs from them.

The criminal justice approach is closely connected to "gun control." Gun use is viewed as a crime problem. Debate focuses on keeping guns out of the hands of criminals and using punishment to deter future gun-related crimes. Solutions often involve punishment as a deterrent for future crimes. A public health approach expands the focus of gun policy beyond keeping guns away from the "bad guys" and addresses the role of guns in suicides, unintentional deaths of children shot by other children, murders among friends and family members, and nonfatal gun injuries.

The mental health approach primarily addresses suicide prevention and deals mostly with individual treatment and care. While this clinical approach is very important for the patient, it is very different from public health's population-based perspective. A clinician treats individuals and provides the best care, through psychotherapy and also at times with medication, possible for them. A public health professional treats the community and may try to change the design and availability of hazardous products such as guns in order to reduce suicide.

Safety education is another approach. It focuses on training individuals in the proper use of guns and educating them about their dangers. This is important and useful and certainly should be done, but safety education has a limited effectiveness with people who are busy, distracted, mentally ill, impulsive, depressed, or under the influence of alcohol or drugs. Public health professionals continue to educate about safe behaviors to prevent injury problems, but have found that education by itself is not enough.

Violence prevention is an evolving set of activities whose object is to prevent or reduce violent behavior. Often this objective is attempted through education and training of individuals to use alternative responses to violent behavior. Learning to control aggressive tendencies might help some individuals who would otherwise use a gun in anger, but, as with safety education, training has limitations and cannot be the only solution to reducing deaths and injuries from firearms.

Public Health Approach:
Injury Control and Product Regulation

Injury control here refers to initiatives by public health workers to prevent injuries or reduce their severity. The scientific study of injuries is relatively new. Both public policy and research on injuries traditionally pointed to the need for individuals to change their behavior rather than to the need to change product design and marketing of hazardous products. However, recently much of the work in injury control related to motor vehicles has focused on improving the design of passenger cars and their roadway environments to reduce the toll of deaths and injuries from motor vehicle crashes. This approach has produced positive results, which compels us to look the same direction when we turn our attention to guns.

An underlying science of injury control is epidemiology. Epidemiologists study the factors that contribute to illnesses and injuries and look for ways to prevent or reduce the outcomes of these factors. Epidemiologists view rather pragmatically the notion of "cause". For them, a cause is something that can be altered to reduce injuries and deaths. For this purpose, it is not necessary to know every link in a causal chain of events to develop successful prevention strategies. We have seen this approach work with injuries from motor vehicle crashes. For example, airbags in passenger vehicles prevent injury in frontal crashes regardless of individual factors: the driver's psychological state, driving skills, or bad luck.

Unfortunately, the epidemiology of deaths and injuries from guns is not as well known as from motor vehicle crashes. As a result, fewer prevention strategies have been scientifically studied. While we present here information from early studies, we do not yet know all the strategies that might be effective for preventing firearm deaths and injuries under the variety of circumstances they occur.

As public health experts, we view the entire community as our patient. We consider all gun related deaths—suicides, homicides, and unintentional acts—to be part of the same problem because, even though the intentions behind each individual act may differ, the gun is common to all. In our society, we need to discuss, research, and evaluate guns and their distribution, just as we do with other consumer products, microorganisms, and environmental agents.

Public health specialists focus on prevention strategies for the community, rather than for the individual. One of the first teachers of injury control principles, Professor Susan Baker from The Johns Hopkins University, commonly used the example of a community's water supply. To prevent water-borne disease, it is more efficient and effective to treat the water supply for the entire community, rather than teach each person to boil water and expect that they would always follow through, although you might also want to teach about boiling water.

Professor Baker, like other injury researchers before her, studies exactly how injuries occur in the body and uses these insights to develop new strategies to prevent injuries or reduce their severity. Colonel John Stapp, another notable figure, presented a compelling example of the power of the injury control perspective. He restrained his body with a seat belt in a rocket sled and demonstrated that properly restrained human beings are capable of withstanding substantial force.[1] Common wisdom in the early 1950s, when Stapp carried out his experiment, was that high forces could cause the body to implode. His work led to the investigation of where injury-causing forces are concentrated in motor vehicle crashes—by objects in the occupant compartment of a car for example. When the human body crashes into these objects at high rates of speed, the impact forces surpass the threshold of human resistance to injury.

Examining the biomechanics of injury forms the basis of injury control. We have found that it is possible to reduce the frequency and severity of injuries even if all injuries cannot be prevented.

Often the best solutions to injury problems are passive ones. William Haddon, Jr., M.D., a founder of modern injury control research, urged public health professionals to focus on changing the product, rather than focusing exclusively on changing individual behavior.[2] When Dr. Haddon did his early work in injury control in the 1960s, motor vehicle crashes were blamed on "the nut behind the wheel." He helped expand the focus and suggested changes in vehicle and roadway design to lessen the intensity of these factors in a crash. He promoted passive or automatic devices that do not require an individual to act each time he or she wants protection. For example, automatic sprinkler systems and fire-retardant building materials will protect people whether or not they have remembered to replace the batteries in smoke detectors, or have memorized an escape route in the case of fire. For products such as cars, passive protection includes airbags, and crush-resistant roofs.

Changing the product often protects people who, for example, forget to fasten their seat belts, good drivers who encounter icy roads, and newly licensed teenagers, as well as careless drivers, and those who are driving too fast. No one deserves death or injury simply because they are humanly careless, forgetful, impulsive, acting on wrong information, or otherwise less than perfect. We believe that our created environment and the products in it should be made to be forgiving, rather than harmful.

There is no single solution to big injury problems.[3, 4] This is certainly true for the deaths and injuries caused by guns; they occur in too many different kinds of situations: an adolescent's suicide, the accidental death of a child who finds and uses a loaded gun, an argument between intoxicated friends that ends in death. Public health professionals do not yet have much information to help develop finely tuned firearm injury control programs. Nevertheless, the work behind policies for other substances, cigarettes, for example, can help guide us in our work for gun policies. The public health community learned to measure the relationship between the type of smoking material (cigars, cigarettes, or pipes), the amount and kind of smoking, and the predicted occurrence of emphysema, lung cancer, and heart disease. This information has helped guide prevention programs and social policies.

When we started studying injury control in the mid-1970s, motor vehicle crashes were the leading cause of death from trauma in the United States. They caused lifelong disabilities in countless people. The work of injury scientists such as Dr. Haddon and Professor Baker helped promote changes in the design of vehicles and in the environment in which vehicles traveled. These changes have helped reduce the number of Americans who die in motor vehicle crashes from over fifty thousand per year in mid-1960s to the current number, about forty thousand per year, even while the number of cars and the miles we drive has increased. In this same time period, however, deaths from guns have increased dramatically: from twenty-eight thousand per year to forty thousand per year. Soon, if current trends continue, guns will surpass motor vehicles as the leading cause of death from trauma in the United States.[5]

The situation is urgent. Much work needs to be done by many people. Our audience for this primer is large—public health professionals, community health advocates, educators, public policy makers, physicians, nurses, criminal justice professionals, and concerned citizens. We expect that each of these groups will take advantage of the insights and information that we provide in this primer. We hope that the injury control perspective will inform their work as they address the issue.

How This Primer Is Organized

Understanding the product associated with deaths and injuries is important to the injury control perspective. Many who are concerned about the problems of firearm deaths and injuries know very little about guns. This primer is a starting place. We want to let our readers know:

THE SCOPE OF THE PROBLEM. Firearm deaths and injuries have become a major public health problem. Firearms are overtaking motor vehicle crashes as the leading cause of injury death in this country. For young black males, firearm homicide is now the leading cause of all deaths. Death rates from firearm homicides have doubled since World War II. But, while many assume the gun problem is about crime, the majority of gun deaths are still from suicide.

HOW GUNS WORK. The desire to make guns more powerful, more accurate, and quicker to load and fire drove the development of guns from early cannons to automatic weapons. These trends continue to influence the guns available today. We describe how guns produce the forces that can result in injury, and describe terms and concepts so that readers can be knowledgeable about different types of guns and ammunition.

HOW GUNS INJURE. We explain the basic biomechanics of how guns produce injuries—the differences between penetrating and per-forating wounds, and the effect of ammunition characteristics.

GUN MANUFACTURE AND GUN SALES. Guns are products that are manufactured, sold, purchased, and used as are other products in our market economy. We describe trends in manufacturing and advertising of guns, including recent ones promoting powerful firearms that are easy to use and easy to conceal. We also describe the legal process for selling guns as well as unregulated gray markets and illegal transfer of weapons.

CURRENT GUN REGULATION. We describe the federal, state, and local laws about guns, concentrating on federal laws and regulations that apply to firearm manufacture. The essence of arguments about the second Amendment and state preemption of local firearm ordinances are also highlighted.

WHAT CAN BE CHANGED. We describe specific measures to reduce firearm injuries through changes in the design and regulation of the gun as a product, methods to change the easy availability of guns and incentives for its use, and product liability litigation.

In each chapter, we have called attention to the public health implications of the many facts we present or the questions that they raise. We have included illustrations and resources to further information. (Footnotes are handled according to American Medical Association style: The numbers in the text refer to a specific same-numbered source note in the appropriate chapter in the "Sources" section, at the end of the book. Footnotes are not, then, numbered sequentially. If you see three numbers listed at the end of a sentence, then each refers to a specific source and all those sources contributed something toward the particular material in the text.)

Too many people are dying and being injured from firearms. Firearms are products that have been neglected in data collection, regulation, and injury research. Guns deserve the same kind of scrutiny that is given to other consumer products. By focusing primarily on the criminal aspects of guns, our society has neglected important policy directions that could address suicides, accidental shootings, and the murder of friends and family members.

Although it is a huge problem, and a complex one, we are optimistic that progress can be made. An injury control perspective has shown us that seemingly intractable social problems can be addressed with sound information, scientific research, and safe product design. We hope this primer will prove to be a useful resource.

REDUCING
FIREARM INJURY
AND DEATH

I

The Scope of the Problem

Firearm deaths and injuries are an enormous burden in the United States. In 1994, firearms are estimated to have killed 39,720 people and injured more than 100,000 others.[1,2] Homicides accounted for 17,190 deaths, suicides for 20,540, and unintentional events for 1,610 deaths. There were an additional 380 deaths of undetermined cause.

Not only are the death statistics alarming, but the costs are immense. The lifetime cost of all firearm injuries, fatal and nonfatal, that occurred in just one year (1990) has been estimated at $20.4 billion.[3]

Deaths from firearms have increased dramatically since World War II. The age-adjusted death rate has doubled for firearm homicides, and has increased by half for firearm suicides (Figure 1.1).[4]

The problem is growing. But its scope has been widely misunderstood because the actions, research, and thinking of public policy professionals have been framed in terms of the circumstances of a shooting, rather than its outcome. Homicides are considered the problem of the criminal justice system, suicides are in the domain of mental health, and unintentional injuries are the concern of safety educators. The science of injury control, however, directs us to look at the product common to all—the gun.

With firearms, the focus is often on fatalities. However, nonfatal firearm injuries are a burden, too, even though we cannot describe the nature and extent of the problem very precisely because there are limited relevant data. In this chapter we present an overview of issues and costs related to fatal and nonfatal firearm injuries.

Firearm Deaths

For many years, firearm suicide, homicide, and unintentional death data were separately collected and coded in national death records.

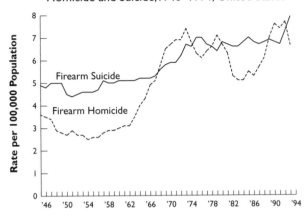

Age-Adjusted Mortality Rates of Firearm
Homicide and Suicide, 1946–1994, United States

FIGURE 1.1 Death rates from firearms have increased significantly since World War II. Homicides from firearms have doubled and suicides from firearms have increased by half. Changes in the age structure of the population are accounted for in these figures. (The mortality data for 1994 are provisional estimates from the National Center for Health Statistics.)

Not until recently have they been reported in the aggregate as "firearm deaths." Even though information on the total burden of firearm fatalities is now more readily available and presents evidence to the contrary, many people still think that the firearm problem is primarily one of homicides. In reality, however, suicide accounts for the majority of firearm deaths, while homicides account for less than half of the firearm deaths each year (Figure 1.2).[1]

Homicides

One reason Americans usually relate firearm injuries to homicides is that United States homicide rates are far greater than those in many other countries (Figure 1.3).[5] In the United States, more than two-thirds of the twenty-three thousand homicides in 1993 were committed with guns (Figure 1.4).[6]

Firearm homicide is most common among young black men (Figure 1.5).[4] In fact, homicide has been the leading cause of death for young black males ages fifteen to nineteen since 1969. For all men in this age group, rates of homicide have almost tripled since the early 1980s. Almost all of this increase is from firearm use.[7]

Although the common fear is of random shootings during robberies, homicides are more likely to occur among friends, families, and acquaintances (Figure 1.6).[6]

Homicides

Suicides

We have less information on suicides than on homicides because for suicides we have to rely solely on what is recorded on the death certificate. About 60 percent of U.S. suicides are committed with firearms. Often, however, all that is recorded is the imprecise term "gunshot wound." We can gather homicide data from both police department records and death certificates.

In Milwaukee County, Wisconsin, where for many years we have been collecting detailed information on the weapons used in firearm suicides and homicides, handguns were the firearms used in 71 percent of suicides.[8] This is similar to the proportion reported (69 percent) in Sacramento County, California, in the early 1980s.[9] There are, however, no data for the nation as a whole.

When people use guns to attempt suicide they are likely to be successful. One study found that 91 percent of all suicide attempts with guns are fatal compared to 23 percent of attempts with drug overdoses.[10]

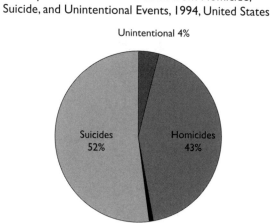

Proportion of Firearm Deaths from Homicide, Suicide, and Unintentional Events, 1994, United States

Unintentional 4%

Suicides 52%

Homicides 43%

Undetermined 1%

FIGURE 1.2 With more than 39,000 deaths attributed to firearms in 1994, more were from suicides than homicides. (The data for 1994 are provisional estimates from the National Center for Health Statistics.)

Suicides from firearms affect a different population than do homicides. The group with the highest risk of firearm suicide is white males over seventy-five years of age (Figure 1.7).[4]

Rates of firearm-related suicide among teenagers are not only much higher than suicides by other means but have increased dramatically, while rates from other methods have increased only slightly (Figure 1.8).[4] More than 80 percent of the rise in suicide rates among teenagers from 1980–1992 was related to firearm use. Guns are used in about 65 percent of youth suicide.[11]

For troubled adolescents, the risk of suicide is 2.5 times higher if there is a gun in the house.[12] In one study that compared households in similar neighborhoods and took into account differences in suicide risk,

4

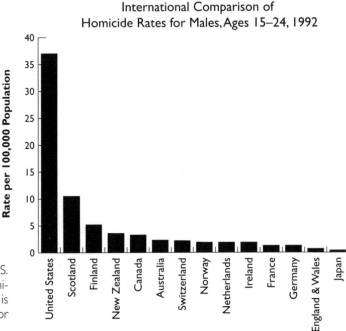

International Comparison of
Homicide Rates for Males, Ages 15–24, 1992

Rate per 100,000 Population

United States · Scotland · Finland · New Zealand · Canada · Australia · Switzerland · Norway · Netherlands · Ireland · France · Germany · England & Wales · Japan

FIGURE 1.3 The U.S. death rate from homicides for young men is much higher than for other countries.

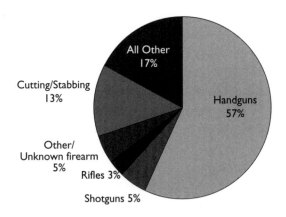

Methods of Homicide, 1993, United States
Uniform Crime Report FBI

All Other 17%

Cutting/Stabbing 13%

Handguns 57%

Other/ Unknown firearm 5%

Rifles 3%

Shotguns 5%

FIGURE 1.4 Of the 23,721 U.S. homicides reported to the FBI in 1993, most were committed with firearms, and handguns are by far the most common firearm used in homicides. (Uniform Crime Report FBI.)

Homicide Rates

Age, Sex, and Race-Specific Incidence Rates of Firearm Homicides, 1994, United States

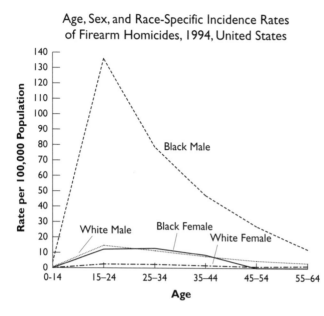

FIGURE 1.5 Young black males are at highest risk for homicide by firearm. Their rates are many times those of other groups at almost all ages.

Relationship of Victim and Perpetrator of Homicides, 1993, United States
Uniform Crime Report FBI

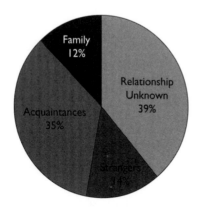

FIGURE 1.6 Of the 23,721 U.S. homicides reported to the FBI in 1993, more murders occurred by family members and acquaintances than by strangers. There were also a large number of homicides where the relationship of the victim and the perpetrator was not known to the police.

Homicide Factors

6   such as medication and alcohol use, the presence of a gun in the home was found to increase the risk of suicide almost 5 times.[13]

Unintentional Events

Our teachers in public health did not refer to unintentional injuries as "accidents." They preferred the term "unintentional injuries" because they said that the term "accident" was often associated with fate or bad luck and thus unpreventable events. We learned from them that "accidents" are generally preventable if the right strategies are applied to the problem.[14]

Unintentional deaths from firearms are much less common than homicidal or suicidal deaths from them. The rate of unintentional firearm deaths has declined substantially since the 1930s. This decline correlates with a decrease in the proportion of Americans who engage in hunting, live in rural areas, and handle guns regularly.[15] In 1994, there were 1,610 such deaths, about 4 percent of all firearm deaths. While still a relatively small part of the firearm problem, this number is larger than unintentional deaths from a number of other causes that

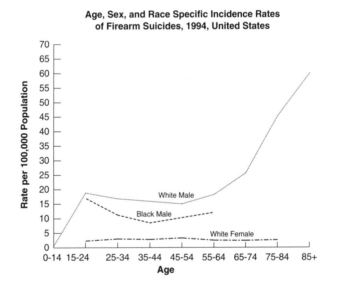

**Age, Sex, and Race Specific Incidence Rates
of Firearm Suicides, 1994, United States**

FIGURE 1.7 The risk of suicide from firearms is greatest for white males over the age of sixty-five. This pattern is quite different from that for homicides from firearms. (Data for 1994 are provisional estimates from the National Center for Health Statistics. Numbers for some groups were too low to generate reliable rate estimates.)

Unintentional Events

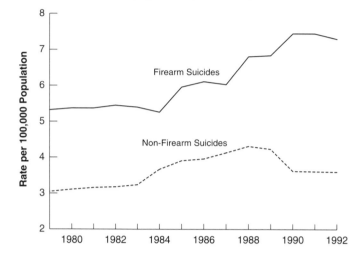

FIGURE 1.8 Over the past decade, teenagers' rates of suicide associated with firearms have been much higher than for suicides by other means, and have increased dramatically over this time.

get far more national focus on prevention. These include deaths related to machinery use (1,037 deaths), collisions between trains and cars (521 deaths), electrocution (525 deaths), and boats (353 deaths/drownings).[4, 16] As with homicides, young black men are at highest risk for unintentional firearm deaths (Figure 1.9).[4]

Firearms and Other Causes of Injuries That Lead to Death

Since the mid-1960s, the rate of deaths resulting from unintentional injuries has decreased steadily, due primarily to the decrease in deaths from motor vehicle injuries. The number of deaths from motor vehicles has dropped from over fifty thousand per year in the early 1970s to about forty thousand in recent years. During this time, deaths from firearms have increased from twenty-eight thousand to forty thousand per year.[16, 17]

If it has not already happened, firearms may soon surpass motor vehicles as the leading cause of death from trauma (Figure 1.10).[4] In nine states—Alaska, Texas, California, Illinois, Louisiana, Maryland, Nevada, New York, and Virginia—and the District of Columbia,

Other Causes

8 firearm deaths outnumbered motor vehicle crash deaths in 1994.[16] In many cities across the country, firearm deaths have outnumbered motor vehicle crashes since the late 1980s.

How Can We Measure the Costs of Firearm Deaths and Injuries?

One estimate of the annual cost in 1990 of deaths and injuries was $20.4 billion.[3] Costs for those surviving their injuries include the costs of medical treatment, of rehabilitation, and of lost wages. Costs also include the value of "foregone productivity," that is, the productivity that the economy has lost when people die too young. Medical costs alone were estimated at $4 billion in 1995.[18]

A recent article traced all the costs of a forty-cent bullet shot with a

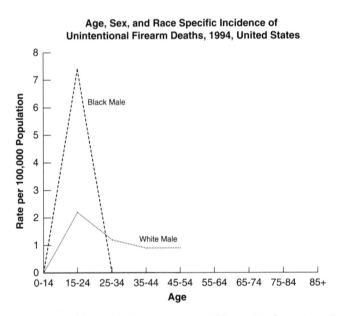

Age, Sex, and Race Specific Incidence of
Unintentional Firearm Deaths, 1994, United States

FIGURE 1.9 Young black males are at highest risk for unintentional deaths from firearms, as they are with homicides from firearms. (Data for 1994 are provisional estimates from the National Center for Health Statistics. Numbers for some groups were too low to generate reliable rate estimates.)

Costs of Firearm Deaths and Injuries

twenty-dollar gun in an assault. The title, "The Two Million Dollar Bullet," nicely sums up the findings. The adult victim sustained a spinal cord injury and lived only a month. Medical expenses accounted for $65,000; life insurance policy payouts amounted to more than $525,000; annual Social Security and worker's compensation pay were $46,000; the criminal justice system expenses were more than $200,000; and lost productivity was estimated to be $1,000,000.[19]

For a very high proportion of firearm injuries, costs for medical care are borne by the public. This occurs not only through taxes for medical assistance programs, but because health care providers shift costs from low reimbursement public programs to other health insurance plans, increasing premiums for all.[19, 20, 21]

Costs can also be estimated with a public health measure called YPLL 65 (for Years of Potential Life Lost before age 65). Deaths from firearms occur in high rates among young people, so by this measure the impact

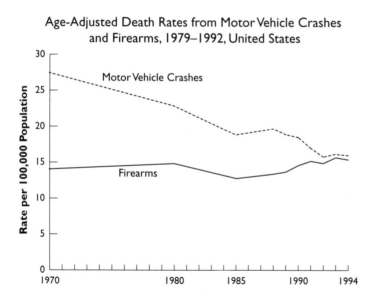

FIGURE 1.10 Age-adjusted death rates from motor vehicle crashes have been decreasing. Death rates from firearms may sometime surpass them. Several states and many cities already have more deaths from gunshot wounds than from motor vehicle crashes. (Data for 1994 are provisional estimates from the National Center for Health Statistics.)

Costs of Firearm Deaths and Injuries

of such deaths is great. The YPLL 65 for any given cause of death is calculated by subtracting the individual's age at death from 65, and summing these years of potential life lost for the population under study.[22]

TABLE 1.1 CHANGES IN YEARS OF POTENTIAL LIFE LOST BEFORE AGE 65[22]

Cause of Death/YPLL	1980 YPLL 65	1991 YPLL 65	% change
Firearms	944,159	1,072,565	+14.0%
Other injuries	2,677,294	2,002,616	-25.2%
Heart disease	1,602,888	1,312,765	-18.1%
Cancer	1,752,730	1,772,010	-1.1%

Nonfatal Injuries

For some events, such as falls, death is an unlikely outcome. Estimates are that sixty-one people are hospitalized and almost nine hundred others sustain injuries per each death from a fall. By contrast, for each death by firearm about three hospitalizations and five other injuries due to firearms are estimated to occur.[23]

While deaths from firearms can be counted from national death certificate data, and the FBI maintains information on homicides from firearms, there is no national registry of all firearm injuries. As a result, we cannot be sure how many people are injured but survive. Special studies, though, estimate that each year almost a hundred thousand people survive shootings long enough to be taken to emergency departments and treated. Of these, nearly 60 percent are injured seriously enough to be hospitalized.[2]

Those who survive firearm injuries are more likely to have been assaulted by another, rather than to have been attempting suicide, if only because most firearm suicide attempts succeed. It is also true that most deaths from firearm injuries are from self-inflicted firearm injuries.

Survival in this instance, however, does not necessarily mean good health. Survivors of firearm injuries may be badly disabled. Nationally,

16.5 percent of spinal cord injuries are caused by gunshots; in some cities the proportion is much higher. In Detroit, for example, the proportion is 40 percent.[24] The proportion for severe brain injury is similar. Individuals with these injuries often require costly medical and rehabilitative care, some for the rest of their lives.

For a variety of reasons, the enormity of this country's firearm death and injury problem has been obscured from public view. Polarized public debates, intense lobbying by pressure groups, widespread misinformation, and lack of knowledge all have contributed toward making this problem seem intractable. But with science, data, and the knowledge and experience of injury control specialists, we can successfully address the problem. Understanding the scope of the problem is the first step.

Nonfatal Injuries

2

Guns and Ammunition—The Basics

In this and the next chapter we present some basic information on what a gun is, how it works, what differentiates one kind of gun from another, and some important things to know about guns and the injuries and deaths they cause. We are not trying to tell you all there is to know about guns. Our goal is to provide you accurate information so you can be conversant about guns and know what terms mean when they are used in gun-related contexts. We point to the characteristics of guns that draw shooters to choose one gun over another, discuss why some guns might be more commonly used than others, and describe what characteristics of guns or their ammunition affect the severity of injury a gun can inflict.

In keeping with the public health perspective of this primer, we spend more time on handguns because they account for the majority of deaths from firearms in this country. We also include some information about shotguns and rifles so you can become familiar with common terms. There is information on the historic development of firearms to help explain what has driven their technologic development. The forces that historically motivated advances in firearm technology are still at work and continue to present new challenges to preventing firearm injury and death. Throughout, we comment on the public health implications of the facts we present.

What Is a Firearm and What Does It Do?

Guns are missile throwers. Throwing objects more effectively means throwing them with greater force, more accuracy, at faster rates, and over longer distances. Whether the object is a stone, spear, arrow, bullet, or some other type of missile, these basic goals motivated every advance in missile-throwing technology. Speed, accuracy, and range, however, have not always completely determined the choice of weapons. For a long time, firearms were inferior to the earlier technology of bows and arrows in those qualities, but these early guns succeeded as weapons because they could be used by people who were weaker and less skilled than archers.[1]

Throughout this primer we use the words gun and firearm as if they were the same, although technically a firearm is a particular kind of gun. A gun is any device that uses pressurized gas or some other form of mechanical energy to force one or more projectiles through a tube and out the end. A firearm is a gun that uses a spark or flame to ignite a powder charge that releases gas as it burns. The gas builds up pressure behind the projectile—usually a bullet—and the pressure forces the projectile through and out the tube.

All firearms are guns, but not all guns are firearms. Some guns use compressed air, carbon dioxide, spring pressure, or even rubber bands to propel their projectiles. A BB gun or an air rifle, for example, uses compressed air to shoot small, round pellets.

Firearms that shoot projectiles with a diameter of 20 mm or less are considered small arms and can usually be fired by one person. Small arms include long guns (rifles and shotguns), which are designed to be held with two hands and fired from the shoulder, and handguns, which are designed to be held and fired with one hand.

Weapons that fire larger projectiles are called artillery. The military has made an arbitrary distinction that weapons which shoot projectiles with diameters greater than 20 mm are artillery. Weapons that fire such large projectiles usually have so much force that the recoil requires some kind of mount or external support for them to be used with any accuracy. Artillery usually must be fired by more that one person, but this distinction is not always true with modern artillery. The artillery category includes bazookas and other types of rocket launchers, and howitzers and other types of cannons.

Cartridges and Bullets

To explain how guns work, we first must introduce ammunition. Although we commonly think of a shooter loading a gun with bullets, this is not technically correct. Instead of bullets, a shooter loads a gun with cartridges. A cartridge is also called a round of ammunition. A

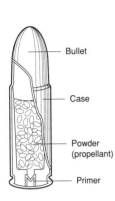

handgun or rifle cartridge consists of a bullet, which is usually made of lead; a powder charge (gun powder) that acts as a propellant by creating gas as it burns; a primer, which is a substance that produces either a flame or a spark to ignite the powder; and a cartridge case to hold all this together. The case for rifle or handgun ammunition is usually made of brass.

FIGURE 2.1 PARTS OF A MODERN CARTRIDGE. Although many people talk about loading a gun with bullets, they really mean cartridges. A cartridge has a bullet, a substance like gun powder to propel the bullet, a primer to ignite the propellant, and a case which holds all these.

Bullet

Case

Powder (propellant)

Primer

For shotguns the projectile is normally a cluster of small, round pieces of metal, or shot, instead of bullets. The shot is housed in a plastic case. Shotgun cartridges are called shells.

The Basic Anatomy of a Firearm

Every handgun has at least three major mechanical parts: the frame, the barrel, and the action assembly.

The frame, or receiver, is a metal housing to which all the other parts are attached. It gives the handgun its basic shape. The rear portion of the frame, called the butt, is turned down, and the grip is attached to the butt. The trigger guard, a loop of metal that surrounds the trigger, is also a part of, or attached to, the frame.

The barrel is the metal tube through which the projectile accelerates. The breech end of the barrel is usually attached to the frame. The muzzle is the open end, from which the bullet exits. The inside surface of the barrel is called the bore.

The action is the mechanical assembly that controls the firing of the gun. It includes, at a minimum, the trigger, the hammer, the firing pin, and the mainspring. On some guns the firing pin is a piece of metal that protrudes between the hammer and where the base of the cartridge rests. On others, the firing pin is a protrusion from the hammer itself. Either way, the purpose of the firing pin is to transfer the force of the falling hammer to the base of the cartridge, igniting the primer and causing the powder to burn. The mainspring returns the hammer back to its resting position against the frame.

For guns that hold many cartridges and that can be fired without reloading, the action also includes the mechanical parts that control the feeding of successive cartridges into the chamber, the part of the gun that holds a cartridge as it is being discharged. Every firearm has at least one chamber.

In general, if a gun can fire more than one shot before reloading, its fourth major component is a place to store multiple cartridges. On most firearms, this is called a magazine. The action feeds successive cartridges from the magazine into the gun's single chamber. Revolvers are an exception, as we will discuss, and have multiple chambers and no magazine.

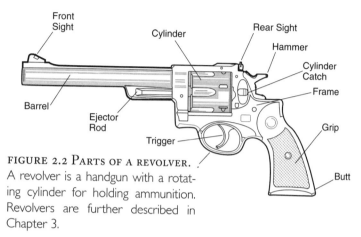

FIGURE 2.2 PARTS OF A REVOLVER. A revolver is a handgun with a rotating cylinder for holding ammunition. Revolvers are further described in Chapter 3.

Rifles and shotguns differ from handguns in that they are designed to be fired from the shoulder and incorporate a stock and a fore-end. The stock is the piece, usually wooden, that houses or surrounds the receiver and gives the rifle most of its shape. The receiver is the part that houses the action. The rear of the stock is called the butt and it rests against the shooter's shoulder. The fore-end, which is also usually made of wood, extends forward and underneath the barrel to give the shooter a place to hold the front of the gun without having to touch the barrel itself. On some historic firearms the action was called a lock; thus the phrase "lock, stock, and barrel," which is still in common use to mean "the whole thing."

How a Gun Works

There are five general steps in firing a typical modern gun: First, a shooter loads a cartridge into the chamber or breech, either by inserting it directly into the firing chamber or by performing a mechanical action to feed a cartridge from a magazine or cylinder into the cham-

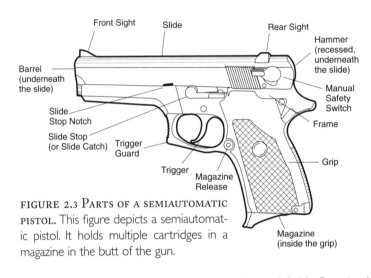

ber. Secondly, the shooter cocks the gun by raising the hammer from its resting place against the frame to a position from which it can drop onto the firing pin. Thirdly, the shooter pulls the trigger, and the gun's mainspring drives the firing pin onto the primer of the cartridge causing the primer to explode and ignite the propellant. The propellant then burns, rapidly releasing gases that expand the cartridge case and force it against the sides of the chamber. Finally the resulting pressure from gas expanding in a closed space forces the bullet through and out of the barrel at a high velocity.

Some firearms harness part of the energy from the firing cartridge and use it to power the action—removing the empty cartridge case from the chamber and feeding a fresh cartridge into the chamber. We discuss this more in Chapter 3, Modern Firearms.

Guns vary greatly in the size of the projectiles they fire and the velocity their projectiles attain. The science of how projectiles perform is called ballistics and is divided into three subfields. Interior ballistics describes what happens to a projectile before it leaves the muzzle of a gun. Exterior ballistics describes the behavior of a projectile as it travels from the gun to the target. Terminal ballistics describes the behavior of the projectile during and after its impact with the target. Wound ballistics is part of terminal ballistics and describes what happens when the target is living tissue. In this book we discuss the interior ballistics of guns in some detail because that is what accounts for their differences in projectile velocity. We do not discuss the exterior ballistics as much because this has greater application to military and hunting uses of weapons. Wound ballistics are described in Chapter 5, Injuries from Firearms.

Front Sight · Slide · Rear Sight · Hammer (recessed, underneath the slide) · Barrel (underneath the slide) · Manual Safety Switch · Slide Stop Notch · Frame · Slide Stop (or Slide Catch) · Trigger Guard · Trigger · Magazine Release · Grip · Magazine (inside the grip)

FIGURE 2.3 PARTS OF A SEMIAUTOMATIC PISTOL. This figure depicts a semiautomatic pistol. It holds multiple cartridges in a magazine in the butt of the gun.

How a Gun Works

For the most part, modern weapons are loaded at the breech, can discharge multiple cartridges before needing to be reloaded, and use as ammunition a self-contained cartridge, with the primer, propellant, and projectile encased in a single unit. However, this has not always been the case. In this section we present a history of firearms to help you understand the design and function of modern weapons and to put into perspective new advances in the accuracy, power, and firing rate of modern guns and ammunition.

Developments in firearms technology have been spurred by a desire to increase the accuracy of weapons, the range over which they could be used, the rate at which they could be fired, and the amount of damage a bullet could inflict on impact. Technological advances typically occur in cycles, with improvements in weapon design opening the door to advances in ammunition technology, and vice versa. Certainly, improvements have been spurred by competitive and self-defense motives. For example, the military of one country adopting a new technology, giving it an advantage over its enemy, would spur the enemy to improve its technology. The history of weapons technology can be seen as a small arms race.[1] While innovations have also been the result of hunters and gunsmiths seeking solutions to their gun problems, widespread implementation of new technologies occurred in the military arena.

Black Powder and Muzzleloaders

Gunpowder, which supplies the propelling force to the bullet, was known in Europe in the thirteenth century and much earlier in the Far East. A German monk is considered by some to have been the first European user. His writings describe how he was able to use the ingredients of black gunpowder—charcoal, salt peter, and sulfur—to blow small rocks and pieces of iron from a basin into the air.[2]

The first firearms were simply miniature cannons: a tube of iron that was closed at one end except for a small hole called a touchhole. Powder and cannon balls were loaded from the muzzle, and a heated wire was inserted into the touchhole. The exploding gunpowder propelled the cannon ball. Hand-held cannons usually were attached to a piece of wood and were held by one person and ignited by another.

A Brief History of Firearm Design

By the late fifteenth century, firearms had progressed to single-person firearms with wooden stocks. These stocks were held against the shoulder, chest, or cheek, and helped the shooter aim the gun and absorb the recoil from the blast. They also provided a fore-end that protected the shooter's hand from the hot metal barrel. A firearm held by one person, rather than a hand cannon that required two to operate, made it possible for a military division to increase its overall rate of fire.

FIGURE 2.4 AN EARLY HAND CANNON (FROM ABOUT 1400). This is a tube of iron that was closed at one end except for a small hole called a touch hole. The tube is fastened onto a wooden club that has an iron spike to steady the whole apparatus against the recoil of firing. A cannon like this would be loaded with gun powder and cannon balls or iron pellets at the muzzle, and ignited at the breech end. (Drawing adapted from *Weapons, An Encyclopedia*.[1])

But early guns were *single-shot* weapons. They could only be discharged once before the shooter had to reload. They were loaded from the muzzle, and the process was slow because the primer, propellant, and projectiles were carried, stored, and loaded separately.

Black gun powder was stored in ammunition pouches or flasks made of horn, wood, or leather. Black powder in any quantity was dangerous because it exploded so easily. When stored in bulk, the risk increased. We still hear as a common English phrase "to go off like a powder keg."

Early bullets were simply round lead balls. Many shooters had their own bullet molds and poured molten lead into them to produce bullets at home.

To speed the laborious process of loading the guns, militaries developed the earliest cartridges—small packages consisting of one bullet, one shot's worth of powder, and a linen or paper wrapper. With the first cartridges, the shooter opened the packages, or cartridges, and loaded the bullet and powder into the muzzle separately. Later versions of muzzleloader cartridges were made with combustible linen or paper, so the shooter could insert the entire unit into the muzzle of the gun.

To load the gun, first the charge of gunpowder (a shot's worth of powder) was poured into the muzzle and a round bullet was inserted into the muzzle. The bullet was pushed firmly down the barrel with a straight metal rod called a ramrod. Then a flat metal pan, called a priming pan, near the breech was loaded with a little more powder and closed. Only then could the weapon be aimed and fired.

Muzzleloaders had a variety of ignition devices. The earliest muzzleloaders, the cannons, were ignited with a lighted rag or torch administered by a second person. Gunsmiths then began to develop ignition devices that required less effort. These ignition devices worked by setting a spark or flame on the small amount of black powder in the priming pan and channeling the resulting explosion through a narrow vent called a flashhole that led to the powder in the barrel. (The spark's effect on the powder in the priming pan is still recalled in the term "flash in the pan.") The matchlock, wheellock, and flintlock are some early ignition systems.

MATCHLOCK. Developed in Europe around 1410, this ignition system was used in Europe until the 1700s, and in Japan and India until the mid-1800s. One type of matchlock had a "reversed-S" shaped piece of metal called a serpentine that held a match, which was a slow-burning rope dipped in salt peter that had one constantly glowing hot end. When the shooter pulled the lower end of the serpentine, the hot end plunged into a pan of powder, igniting the explosion. This primitive trigger device allowed the firearm to be fired with one finger, leaving both hands and arms free to steady the weapon, aim it, and absorb the recoil.

WHEELLOCK. This ignition system was first developed by Leonardo da Vinci around 1500. A serrated wheel of the wheellock turning against iron pyrite created sparks for the primer. It was too complex and too expensive to be used by rank-and-file military, but the wheellock technology helped make it easier for horse riders to use pistols because they could fire them with one hand.

FLINTLOCK. Flintlock weapons were first demonstrated around 1620, and by the early 1700s the flintlock made the matchlock obsolete in Europe. It used a flint scraping on steel to create a shower of sparks that ignited the powder in the priming pan. The flint usually lasted about twenty shots before it had to be replaced.

In addition, they used black powder, which was smoky and fouled the gun's barrel, the breech, and the ignition mechanisms. To function well, firearms had to be cleaned frequently, further impeding speed.

Black Powder and Muzzleloaders

20 Black powder was not an efficient propellant. When it exploded, only about half of its mass helped propel the bullet. The rest turned to smoke and soot. The powder smoke from the priming pan and the muzzle also blocked the shooter's vision, making it difficult to aim the next shot. The primer also sometimes flashed backward, injuring the shooter. The term "backfire" can be traced to this.

The muzzleloaders were all single-shot weapons and slow to load. Despite its problems, the single-shot black powder muzzleloader was the weapon of choice for nearly four centuries—from the middle 1400s to the 1850s.

Rifling

Typically, the diameter of the muzzleloader's round bullet was about one millimeter smaller than the diameter of the bore. Because the bullet did not form a tight seal with the firearm's smooth bore, expanding gas from the propellant escaped through the gap between

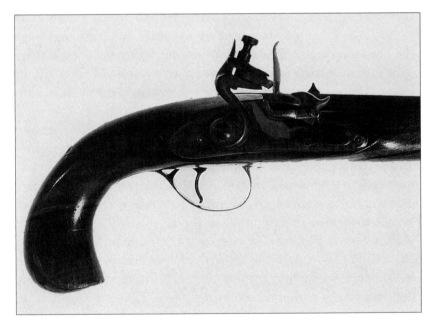

FIGURE 2.5 A FLINTLOCK FIRING MECHANISM ON AN OLD PISTOL. The flint is held in a clamp and, when the trigger is pulled, the flint scrapes against the metal, creating sparks to ignite the priming powder. Flints had to be replaced after about twenty shots. This pistol dates from around 1820.

the bore and the bullet. Thus, less pressure could be applied to the bullet itself. The gap between the bore and the bullet also made the flight of the bullet rather inaccurate because the bullet's direction of departure could vary widely.

A larger bullet formed a tighter seal against the bore, but was more difficult to ram down the barrel during loading. In the mid-1500s, gunsmiths began to make guns with straight grooves in the bore. Bores with straight grooves made it easier to load the gun with a larger bullet. With a tighter seal against the bore, the larger bullets made these guns more accurate than smooth-bore firearms.

Two centuries later, in the mid-1700s, shooters and gunsmiths hypothesized that helical or spiral grooves in the bore might give a gyroscopic spin to a bullet that would stabilize its flight and further increase the firearm's accuracy. The hypothesis proved to be correct: The bullet acquired its spin by rubbing against the raised areas between the grooves, called lands, as it accelerated through the barrel.

A bore with lands and grooves is called a rifled bore, and the lands and grooves themselves are called rifling. Starting in the mid-1700s, helical grooves entirely replaced straight grooves. Today, the term rifle is used for a long arm with lands and grooves in its bore. Long arms with smooth bores were commonly called muskets. Long arms are not the only modern firearms with rifled bores; handguns have rifled bores too.

Rifles were widely used during the American Revolution, but did not immediately replace smooth-bore guns as the firearm of choice. Rifled barrels and bullets that were the diameter of the bore improved the accuracy of firearms and made it possible for them to fire larger bullets, but these guns remained difficult to load. After the introduction of helical rifling in the mid-1700s, a century passed before its greatest effect on firearm accuracy, power, and range could be realized.

Loading, Igniting, and Cartridge Systems

In addition to their other drawbacks, the matchlock and flintlock were difficult to use in wet weather because the primer would not ignite as easily. By the end of the 1700s, materials that exploded on impact were discovered, and shortly afterwards, in 1808, a Scottish pastor, named Dr. Alexander Forsyth, invented percussion ignition. He was fond of duck hunting and wanted to enjoy his sport in wet weather.[2] Percussion ignition involved the use of chemical detonating compounds and a trigger-activated hammer that crushed and ignited them. The hammer and detonating compounds together produced the flash that ignited the gunpowder. Earliest percussion compounds were contained in a glass scent bottle affixed to the side of the gun.

Percussion ignition was simplified with the development of percussion caps in 1818. A percussion cap also contained a chemical compound that created a spark when struck. Percussion caps were first used with muzzle-loaders; they fit over the flashhole, replacing the priming pan. When the caps were hit with a hammer, the resulting explosion flashed down the flashhole to ignite the gunpowder charge behind the bullet. These caps became widely used, and by 1840 the military began replacing the flintlock system with the percussion ignition system because of its reliability.

Percussion caps paved the way for the development of a self-contained cartridge that included a percussion igniter (primer), propellant, and projectile in a single case. Early cartridge cases were made of linen or paper, but as the manufacturing capacity of the Industrial Revolution increased, metallic cartridges of brass were soon easily and cheaply made. The self-contained cartridge paved the way for the development of practical breech-loading firearms.

Loading from the muzzle had always impeded the speed of fire, and gunsmiths had struggled for centuries to create an effective alternative. Breech loaders, guns that could be loaded at the breech end of the barrel rather than from the muzzle, were desirable in situations when it was impractical to ram a charge down the barrel when, for example, the shooter was behind cover, on horseback, or lying down. However, gunsmiths had found it difficult to overcome the problems of misfires and explosions in a gun where gunpowder was both loaded and ignited at the breech. It was also hard to build breech loaders so that the exploding gases did not escape through the cracks in the breech needed for the loading mechanisms. This escaping gas diminished the bullet's velocity, which in turn diminished the firearm's range and accuracy. It was also dangerous to the shooter, posing a risk of injury from burning gases directed at the face. Several early attempts at breech-loading flintlocks were either failures or too expensive to manufacture for use by the common soldier.

Loading, Igniting

Development of a self-contained cartridge, with the primer included, made it possible to produce accurate breech loaders with a greater range than was previously possible with muzzle-loading small arms. Self-contained cartridges also reduced the problem of gas escaping at the breech, because the metal case expanded against the sides of the chamber as the shooter fired the gun. With the breech sealed this way, all of the pressure from the expanding gas could be applied in the forward direction, although some gas still escaped through the gap between the bore and the bullet. Although reloading was faster than for the muzzleloader, these early breech-loading weapons were still single shots. Inventors and gunsmiths struggled with making multiple-shot weapons. The most common devices increased the number of barrels. Double-barreled weapons are still made, but there were also early weapons made with six or seven barrels. These were the precursors to the modern revolver.

Revolvers and Repeaters

Revolvers are handguns with rotating cylinders. The term pistol has come to mean handguns other than revolvers, but the first revolvers were simply modifications of the pistol. Pistols were used early on as defensive weapons because of their convenience, but the military concentrated on long arms for military engagements because pistols were less accurate and had a shorter range. Horseback riders, especially, used the pistol because it could be fired with one hand while the other hand held the reins. Early pistols were muzzle loaded and slow to reload. To compensate, some gunsmiths added extra barrels to the gun, or people carried two guns. Still, the shooter had to reload after discharging the one cartridge that had been loaded into each barrel of each gun.

Revolvers developed out of the desire to have multiple shots available. Early revolvers were muzzleloaders with multiple revolving barrels. Percussion ammunition made revolver technology easier than the more cumbersome flintlock and wheellock actions. For a time, pepperbox revolvers, so named because of their resemblance to pepper containers of the era, with six or seven revolving barrels were popular. There were even revolving muskets and rifles. Samuel Colt developed his more familiar revolver, with a short revolving cylinder capable of holding six cartridges, and one barrel, in 1835.

24   Colt's innovation was to make a revolving cartridge holder, the cylinder, and connect its rotation with the action of the hammer. As the hammer was pulled back, or cocked, the cylinder rotated. Then, when the trigger was pulled, the hammer struck the previously loaded percussion cap that ignited and propelled the bullet. The bullet and propellant were loaded from the muzzle end of the cylinder, and percussion caps were loaded from the breech end.

Once metal cartridges were widely available in the mid-nineteenth century, breech-loading revolvers were developed by Colt, Smith & Wesson, and other manufacturers. The essential design of the revolver has not changed since then, although the metals and the alloys used today may be different.

Single-shot, breech-loading long arms were widely used by militaries throughout the last half of the nineteenth century. Many of the designs were simple, accurate, and reliable, and are still used today in guns for target shooting and hunting. Ruger rifles and Browning rifles are two examples. But the armies of the world sought faster rates of fire, and the metal cartridges that advanced the technology of breech loading also spurred the development of "repeaters" for long arms in the latter half of the nineteenth century.

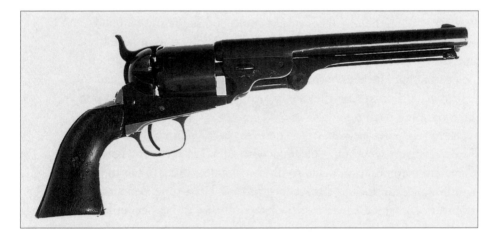

FIGURE 2.6 A COLT REVOLVER FROM 1880. Early revolvers held six cartridges in the cylinder. This decreased the time it took to reload. Previously, single-barreled pistols were reloaded after each shot.

Revolvers and Repeaters

A repeater is any gun that can fire more than one shot between reloadings. Revolvers with their multichambered cylinders and guns with multiple barrels were the earliest repeaters. But metallic cartridges made it possible to develop repeating arms with a single chamber and a single barrel. Such a repeater has a mechanism that feeds cartridges into the chamber before firing and extracts empty cases from the chamber after firing. A gun with this kind of repeating action stores cartridges in a part of the firearm called the magazine. On some firearms, the magazine is a tube on the underside of the barrel. On others it may be a cavity in the handle or the butt of the weapon, or in a box near the breech.

A manual repeater is a gun whose mechanical action must be manually operated by the shooter. The manual repeating actions developed in the nineteenth century are still used today. (See Chapter 3, Modern Firearms, for a description of repeating action on long arms.)

Types of Bullets and Gunpowder

Breech loaders, self-contained cartridges, and repeating actions contributed greatly to increases in firing rates. But, as with many advances in firearms technology, their widespread acceptance did not occur immediately. During the first half of the nineteenth century, the French Army was still using muzzle-loaded, single-shot rifles, and elongated bullets. The army had overcome some of the difficulty of loading these firearms, but an officer named Claude Minié developed a solution that further advanced gun technology.

Although early rifle bullets were round, the gyroscopic spin created by the rifled bores had paved the way for an important advance in firearms and ammunition: elongated bullets. Given a fixed-bore diameter, the only way to make a bullet bigger and heavier was to make it longer. But these elongated bullets were not accurate in smooth-bore muskets because, without a spin around its long axis, an elongated bullet was not aerodynamically stable and did not fly point first.

Minié created elongated bullets with a diameter slightly smaller than the gun's bore. The bullet was also slightly conical, with a broader base and narrower nose. Its most important feature, though, was the hollow, concave indentation in its base. When the propellant ignited, its expanding gases forced the bullet's sides outward at the base, making a tight fit against the rifled bore. Unlike a round ball, the bullet did not need to be pounded down several times in order to get its base snug at the bottom of the barrel when loaded through the muzzle, so it retained its shape during loading. The elongated bullet had a tighter fit within the barrel and better contact with the rifling, so that more of the expanding gases worked to propel the bullet. As the elongated bullet is more aerodynamically stable, the higher velocity projectiles meant more accurate firearms with greater ranges.

This development spurred other changes. The soft lead bullets could not withstand the increased explosive forces needed to propel the heavier bullets. Instead of being lightly rifled by the grooves in the bore, bullets were now being damaged in the gun's barrel. Soon, manufacturers created bullets with a coating of harder metal over the full length of the bullet—the so-called "full-metal jacket" over a lead inner core.

This technology of higher powered, fully jacketed bullets was aided by other advances in ammunition: nitrocellulose, or gun cotton, and Alfred Nobel's related invention of a smokeless gunpowder made of nitroglycerin derivatives. A major difference between black powder and smokeless powder was that smokeless powder burned in a controllable manner, whereas black powder exploded. The new powder decreased the smoke and reduced fouling of the gun mechanisms. Because the powder burned more efficiently, more of the powder burned to release pressurized gas and thus more pressure against the bullet was created. The powder could also be made in grains of specific shapes and sizes. This allowed some control over the speed at which the powder would burn. By varying the quantity of powder and the speed at which it burned, manufacturers could create cartridges that maximized the propellant's ability to accelerate a bullet through the barrel.

Soft-Point and Hollow-Point Bullets

Fully jacketed bullets and repeating long arms were in widespread use by military forces in the late 1800s. During a battle in India in 1895, the British Army decided that full-metal jacket projectiles, in spite of their relatively high muzzle velocities, were not effective enough in stopping enemy soldiers. They requested help from an ammunition factory in Dum Dum, India, and were given a metal jacketed bullet with the top of the jacket ground off so that a small amount of lead was exposed at the bullet's point. This modified projectile was the first of what have come to be known as soft-point bullets. Whereas a fully jacketed bullet might travel completely through a body and create only a small hole, a soft-point bullet expanded on impact. The expanded bullet dissipated more energy in the body, creating a larger wound. A British laboratory improved on the soft-point design and created bullets with a small hole in the nose (hollow-point) which would also expand on entering the target. The British Army used these hollow-point and soft-point bullets in military engagements during 1897 and 1898, finding that they caused more casualties than fully jacketed bullets. In modern usage, any of the expanding bullets, soft-point and hollow-point bullets being two examples, are commonly called dum dum bullets. Because the wounds they made were thought to be especially inhumane, international law outlawed their use by the military in 1899. (See Chapter 5, Injuries from Firearms, for a discussion of the wounding potential of fully jacketed versus hollow-point bullets.)

Improving the loading and firing speed of guns, increasing the accuracy of the bullet, and maximizing the wounding power of the bullet have driven the development of firearms and ammunition throughout history. Such developments also apply to contemporary firearms and ammunition. We turn our attention to modern firearms in the next chapter, after presenting some basic concepts that will be important for that discussion.

Common Terms for Guns and Ammunition

This section describes some common terms that people use when discussing guns. We emphasize those which are relevant to considering firearm injuries and death from a public health perspective.

Caliber

Caliber is a term that applies to both guns and ammunition. In the most general sense of the term, the caliber of a bullet is its diameter and the caliber of a gun, either a handgun or a rifle, is the diameter of the inside of the barrel—the bore diameter. Every gun has a fixed diameter for its bore and fixed dimensions for its chamber. A gun can only fire bullets whose diameter is the same as its bore diameter, so, the caliber of a gun is the same as the caliber of the bullets it is designed to fire. Caliber is measured in millimeters or fractions of an inch. Among common types of ammunition, the smallest bullets for handguns and rifles are .22 caliber or 22/100ths of an inch in diameter. Some less commonly used rifles fire .17 caliber bullets. Two common handgun calibers are 9 mm and .380. They are approximately the same, but 9 mm is a metric measure and slightly larger than the .380. They are not interchangeable.

As stated above, the firearm's caliber designation is usually the same as the physical diameter of its bore, but sometimes the caliber is a nominal diameter that differs slightly from the physical diameter. For example, the bore diameter of the .357 Magnum revolver is .357 inches, but so is the bore diameter of the .38 Special revolver.

There are dozens of different weapon calibers, but some are more common than others. Manufacturers make handguns in approximately ten common calibers and rifles in approximately twenty common calibers.

In general, the caliber of a gun has been roughly correlated with its overall size, although there are some important exceptions. A gun that effectively shoots large bullets must itself be bigger than a gun that shoots small bullets. With smaller calibers not only is the bullet smaller, but the powder charge needed to propel the bullet is smaller as well. A gun that shoots large-caliber bullets must be manufactured to withstand the forces generated by the larger powder charge required to propel the bigger bullet.

Caliber, as it correlates with the overall weight of a bullet, determines how much energy a bullet acquires before leaving the muzzle of a gun, and therefore, how much energy the bullet has when it enters the body.

Although most large-caliber guns are bigger and heavier than most small-caliber guns, a recent trend in the manufacture of firearms is the use of materials and designs that allow for large-caliber handguns that are relatively small in size.[3, 4] Typically, a large-caliber cartridge generates more recoil, and a heavier gun reduces the amount of recoil that is transferred to the shooter's arm. Shooters who want better control of a large-caliber firearm may favor heavier and bigger guns. But others with an interest in carrying a smaller, lighter firearm may favor smaller and lighter guns.

Caliber

Generally speaking, as it exits the muzzle of a gun, a small bullet fired from a small gun has less energy than a large bullet from a large gun. Although a bullet's lethality is not directly correlated with its energy, the amount of tissue damage a bullet can inflict is determined in part by how much energy a bullet has when it strikes the body. (See Chapter 5.) All other things being equal, the potential to inflict tissue damage is greater with a larger caliber gun and bullet than a smaller caliber gun and bullet. All other things are, however, seldom equal. A small-caliber gun is still a lethal one. Many of the cheapest guns available have traditionally been small-caliber ones. Their price has made them easier to acquire, and their small size makes them easy to conceal.[3] There is a trend, discussed in Chapter 6, toward the manufacture of inexpensive large-caliber guns, as well as small-sized large-caliber guns.[4] The combination of large caliber, small size, and inexpensive price is a troubling one. We do not have the necessary public health surveillance systems in place to document whether deaths and injuries change as a result of this trend.[5, 6] With other products, motor vehicles for example, we are able to track both the product and deaths and injuries associated with the products. This information helped to identify, for example, that in crashes, small cars are more likely to be associated with serious occupant injuries and that, as the proportion of small cars on the road increased, the number of deaths and severe injuries did as well.[7]

Caliber is one piece of information that forensic scientists use in trying to match a bullet to the gun that fired it. If a doctor or medical examiner recovers a bullet from the body of a shooting victim, forensic scientists can determine its caliber and begin to narrow their search for a weapon. Although the caliber alone is not enough to establish a link between a bullet and a gun, the caliber must match before a link can be established. To establish a conclusive link, forensic scientists use other distinctive markings on the bullet.

Cartridge Designations

There are hundreds of different kinds of ammunition available. When a shooter purchases ammunition, caliber is important in determining what to buy, but caliber alone does not determine all. A cartridge type is a combination of a caliber, such as .357, and a manufacturer's designation, such as Magnum. In the same vein, .38 is a common caliber for revolvers, and .38 Special is a common cartridge type.

Naming conventions are not consistent. Sometimes they denote the make of the gun for which the ammunition was developed, such as .38 S&W for Smith & Wesson, or .45 ACP for Automatic Colt Pistol. Others, originally coined when shooters used black powder, indicate the weight of the original black powder charge in grains, even though black powder has not been used in decades. For example, a .45-70-405 cartridge is 0.45 inches in diameter, has the equivalent charge of 70 grains of powder, and has a bullet that weighs 405 grains (436 grains = one ounce).

Cartridges vary by the length of the case, the design of the base, the type of primer, the type and quantity of powder they use, and the size,

FIGURE 2.7 SOME COMMON CARTRIDGES. From left to right .22; .22 LR; 9 mm short; 9 mm Parabellum; .38; .357; .44; .223 Remington; 30-06. Twenty-two's are used in both handguns and rifles. The .223 Remington and 30-06 are rifle ammunition. The other cartridges are for handguns. The .38, .357, and .44 are "hollow-points". Other differences are described in the text.

Cartridge Designations

TABLE 2.1 COMMON HANDGUN AND RIFLE CARTRIDGES

Cartridge Name	Type of Firearm	Comments
.22 rimfire	revolver, pistol, and rifle	The smallest caliber cartridge in common use. The .22 Long Rifle (or .22 LR), a cartridge in this family, is one of the most popular of all firearm cartridges.
.357 Magnum	revolver	A gun that chambers this cartridge can also chamber .38 Specials, but the reverse is not true. The Magnum has an extra powder load and is essentially an elongated .38 Special cartridge.
.38 Special	revolver	"Special" refers to an increase in power required for revolvers. The .38 Special was for many years the most common service revolver for law enforcement agents.
.44 Magnum	revolver	The Magnum designation has come to be associated with extra power.
.25 ACP	pistol	ACP stands for Automatic Colt Pistol, as this cartridge was first manufactured for a Colt firearm.
.32 ACP	pistol	ACP stands for Automatic Colt Pistol.
.380 ACP (9 mm short)	pistol	A .380 bullet is similar in size to a 9 mm, but the cartridge case is shorter. As a result, the .380 ACP is less powerful than the standard 9 mm. In other countries this cartridge is sometimes referred to as a 9 mm short.
9 mm Parabellum	pistol	Parabellum is Latin, meaning "for war." It differentiates 9 mm Parabellum cartridges from 9 mm Short cartridges. Another term for this cartridge is the 9 mm Luger, as the term was first used by the German manufacturer of the Luger pistol.
.40 S&W	pistol	S&W refers to Smith & Wesson.
.45 ACP	pistol	ACP stands for Automatic Colt Pistol.
.30-06	rifle	06 refers to 1906, the first year of its production.
.30-30	rifle	The second "30" refers to the original weight of black powder propellant in grains

Cartridge Designations

shape, and weight of the bullet. Some cartridge designations provide information about the physical characteristics of the cartridge itself. For example, the .22 short, and the .22 long are both .22 caliber cartridges, but the latter has a longer cartridge case and more propellant. But not all cartridge designations reflect the cartridge's heritage or physical characteristics. Some are merely industry standards that have come to be associated with a combination of physical and practical characteristics. For example, a .44 Magnum revolver uses .44 caliber bullets and the Magnum indicates they have extra powder (hence power) for their size. The .357 Magnum has fast-burning powder and a case that is designed to withstand the greater pressure that the propellant creates as it burns.

A shooter commonly speaks not only of a firearm's caliber but also its chambering, which is the type of cartridge its chamber is manufactured to accommodate. As a rule, a firearm can discharge only a single type of cartridge, but there are a few exceptions. One notable exception is the .357 Magnum revolver, which can also fire .38 Special cartridges.

Cartridges generally are designed for use in one type of firearm—pistol, revolver, or rifle—but not others. There are, however, some cartridges that may be used in more than one type of firearm. Table 2.1 is a list of some common cartridges and the types of firearms in which they are most commonly used. One cartridge, the .22 rimfire, is widely used in revolvers, pistols, and rifles.

A blank is a cartridge that does not contain a bullet. It contains a powder charge, but either the case is crimped at the neck where the bullet should be, or the bullet is replaced by a felt and paper wad. A blank is meant to produce noise only, but the resulting blast of gas can kill or cause injury if discharged close enough to a vulnerable anatomic site such as the head. Blanks are primarily used for training.

A dummy is a cartridge that does not contain a live primer or a powder charge. Dummies are used instead of live cartridges for testing the mechanical function of the firearm and in various training applications.

Rimfire and Centerfire Cartridges

Cartridges vary in where their primer is located. Rimfire cartridges are those that hold the detonating compound in a rim around the base of the cartridge case. Louis Flobert, the French gunsmith who first developed this type of cartridge, reshaped the percussion cap in use at the time, gave it a rim, and then loaded it with a small round lead bullet. He included no other powder charge, because the primer itself had enough explosive force to propel the bullet. When the gun's hammer dropped from the cocked position, it crushed the rim of the cartridge and detonated the primer. This ammunition was used for indoor target shooting, or parlor shooting, a sport that became very popular in some parts of Europe in the 1840s.[2]

Smith & Wesson, an American gun and ammunition manufacturing company, went on to devise and patent a .22 caliber rimfire cartridge that was like Flobert's, but also contained a powder charge. This ammunition was developed in 1857 and is still in use today.

The rimfire cartridge case cannot be too thick or it will prevent the falling hammer from crushing the rim and detonating the primer. However, the thin cartridge case makes this design too weak for larger powder charges which generate chamber pressures beyond what the case can withstand. The most common rimfire ammunition in general use today is .22 caliber.

The cartridge case's thin rim also meant that the primer compound was exposed and relatively unprotected, making the cartridges vulnerable to accidental detonation when they were heavily jostled. This was especially a problem in carrying cartridges. To get around this problem, manufacturers sought a way to locate the primer in a less vulnerable part of the cartridge. This led to the development of the first centerfire cartridge in the mid-nineteenth century. With the centerfire cartridge, the primer is a percussion cap located in the center of the cartridge's base. When a shooter fires a centerfire gun, the hammer pushes the firing pin into the center, not the rim, of the cartridge's base. The case can be thicker and stronger than with the rimfire cartridge. Except for the .22 caliber, most handguns and rifles use centerfire ammunition.

Public Health Implications: The historical development of rimfire and centerfire ammunition demonstrates that ammunition can be, and in fact has been, modified to produce a wide range of effects, some of them less lethal and more safe than others. Rimfire ammunition for indoor sport used a light bullet and no powder charge,

Rimfire and Centerfire Cartridges

resulting in bullets that traveled at relatively low velocities. Center-fire ammunition developed, in part, because rimfire ammunition could be detonated accidentally: a technologic response to a perceived safety problem. The solution to contemporary problems of firearm deaths and injuries may also involve modifying ammunition. The technological changes may not be very difficult, but agreeing on the desired outcome for ammunition use—stunning, but not killing, for example—may prove to be difficult. Nonetheless, there are models to turn to: Law enforcement agencies in some countries such as Israel and Ireland make routine use of non-lethal rubber ammunition, although the caliber of that ammunition (40 mm) exceeds the 20 mm diameter that traditionally distinguishes small arms from artillery.[2]

Cartridge Cases

Beyond containing the projectile, powder charge, and primer, the cartridge case performs an important function in the firing process. To maximize the explosive force of the bullet, the rear of the combustion chamber must be completely sealed so the gases can propel the bullet at maximum velocity in one direction. The case creates this seal when the burning propellant's expanding gases press the external side of the case against the wall of the chamber. This seal also protects the gun's action from the corrosive effects of the gases.

Bullet Designs and Materials

A bullet can be classified according to its shape, or some other aspect of its design, and the material with which it is constructed. Common terms are described below. They are often used in conjunction with one another.

PROJECTILE SHAPE. Projectiles (bullets) are generally conical in shape. The forward portion of a bullet is commonly called its nose. Handgun bullets have many different nose configurations. A rifle bullet tends to be longer, with a more pronounced point at the nose. This streamlined shape is aerodynamically suited for traveling the longer distances over which rifles are more commonly fired.

MATERIAL. Most bullets are made of lead, or have a lead core. A full-metal jacket bullet is usually comprised of a lead core covered

completely with a thin coating of another metal, usually copper. The
full-metal jacket keeps the lead core from shredding or melting during
discharge and fouling the interior of the rifled barrel. Some bullets are
semi-jacketed, with the lead core exposed at the bullet's nose. A semi-
jacketed bullet is also called a soft-point bullet. Bullets that have a harder
core such as of steel or tungsten are also manufactured. They are specifically for defeating armor for military or police use. Hard-core handgun
ammunition was banned from manufacture for the civilian population
in the United States in 1986. These are the so-called "armor-piercing"
bullets. When fired at a high velocity, they can sometimes penetrate
vehicles and protective devices such as body armor (bullet-proof vests).
They are also called hard-core or steel-core bullets.

DESIGN. Some bullets are specially designed and constructed to
produce a characteristic effect on impact. Hollow-point bullets are an
example. They are either fully jacketed or semi-jacketed with a hollow
tip—a hole drilled in the bullet's nose—so that they expand on impact.
Sometimes this expanding effect is called mushrooming because the
expanded bullet resembles a mushroom. This kind of deformation
increases the tissue damage in the body. Controlled-expansion bullets,
of which the Winchester Silver Tip (also called the Black Talon) is one
example, also deform. Rather than random mushrooming, these bullets
expand to a predictable, predesigned shape on impact, the nose
splaying with a certain number of protrusions. The Black Talon is
unique because its star-shaped pattern results in razorlike edges and
points (see Figure 5.3).

Exploding or incendiary bullets carry explosive devices under the
bullet jacket. On impact, these will explode or burn and are usually targeted at military objectives, not humans or animals. Tracer bullets carry
a pyrotechnic substance in a hole or cup at the rear of the bullet which
burns in flight to illuminate their trajectory. Fragmenting bullets are
designed to break into pieces on impact, creating multiple projectiles
that act like independent missiles within the target. One such bullet
consists of a cluster of shotgun pellets inside a metal jacket covered at
the nose by a plastic cap. The tissue damage from this bullet can be
extensive. These bullets can be purchased by civilians.

Rifle bullets for hunting animals, on the other hand, are required to be
hollow point or soft point. When full-metal jacket bullets hit an animal,

they can easily pass through, creating entrance and exit wounds and leaving internal injuries without causing death. Because it is believed that this would prolong the suffering of the wounded animal, hollow-point or soft-point bullets are used in order to kill the animal quickly.

Bullet Designs and Materials

3

Modern Firearms

In this section we describe how modern guns work, how they are loaded, what kind of ammunition they use, and how much they cost. A gun's physical characteristics influence its range and accuracy and the velocity of its projectiles. This in turn influences how manufacturers market guns and how consumers choose a gun that meets their perceived needs. Although any gun can produce a lethal wound, a gun's physical characteristics also influence its wounding potential. Its action and the speed at which it can be loaded influence the speed at which it can fire successive shots. A firearm's cost influences its availability and distribution which are critical factors in understanding the epidemiology of firearm injury and death.

Many of the historic firearm designs discussed in the Chapter 2 are still used in gun manufacture in the United States. Patterns of manufacture, distribution of firearms, and their ownership in the U.S. population are discussed in Chapter 6, Where Guns Come From.

Derringers

Henry Deringer was an American gunsmith in the mid-nineteenth century who developed a muzzle-loaded single-shot pistol that was small enough to be carried in a trousers or vest pocket, or a boot. His invention has come to be known as the derringer, in a variation on the spelling of his name. A derringer is a handgun with no magazine and no cylinder. It has no place to store a cartridge except in the chamber. However, a derringer may have multiple chambers with a separate barrel for each. Two-shot derringers are the most common variety, but there are also single-shot, four-shot, and other types. Derringers are still manufactured, but in smaller numbers than other pistols.

The technical term for a revolver is a pistol revolver, to distinguish it from a semiautomatic pistol. As a rule, revolvers do not have manual safety devices, but some modern revolvers have design features that are intended to reduce the risk of accidental discharge. Unlike pistols and rifles, most revolvers cannot be completely sealed at the breech between barrel and cylinder because of their loading mechanisms. This results in some gas leakage between the forward end of the cylinder and the rear of the barrel.

How a Revolver Works

A revolver is a manual repeater. It fires one bullet with each trigger pull and must be cocked each time it is to be fired. The revolver has a rotating cylinder, typically with six chambers, where the cartridges rest waiting to be fired. As the shooter fires the gun the cylinder rotates to line up each chamber, in succession, with the hammer and the barrel. Revolvers were the most common handguns for much of the twentieth century. The revolver's design is mechanically simple, thereby minimiz-

FIGURE 3.1 A DERRINGER. First developed in the mid-nineteenth century, the derringer is a handgun with no magazine and no cylinder. It was the first popular small pistol and was referred to as a "pocket pistol." This derringer has two barrels and is a double shot.

ment by semiautomatic pistols as the weapon of choice among law
enforcement agents, until recently.

One way to understand the difference between single-action
revolvers and double-action revolvers is to think of the firing process
as having two stages. Given a loaded gun, it must be first cocked and
then discharged. With a single-action revolver, the shooter manually
cocks the gun by raising the hammer; after that, a pull of the trigger
discharges the gun. To fire consecutive shots, the shooter manually
cocks the gun before each shot. With a double-action revolver, the
shooter pulls the trigger to both cock and discharge the firearm. To fire
consecutive shots, the shooter just pulls the trigger again and again.
The term action refers not to what the shooter does but rather to what
the gun does in response to a pull of the trigger.

To fire a single-action revolver, the shooter applies one to five
pounds of pressure to the trigger. To fire a double-action revolver, the
shooter applies about twelve to fifteen pounds of pressure. It takes this
much force to cock the weapon (raise the hammer) before it can be
discharged. The application of this force can cause the shooter to move
the barrel slightly during firing, which may adversely affect the shooter's
ability to place a bullet at its intended target. However, most double-
action revolvers can also be fired in single-action mode after being
manually cocked; less trigger pressure is required to discharge the gun
in single-action mode.

Some single-action revolvers have a half-cock position in the hammer.
This is a notch designed to catch the hammer if it slips from the thumb
as it is being cocked. A gun carried in a half-cocked position can sometimes discharge unintentionally when dropped—the hammer is jarred
free of the notch and fires the revolver. Thus the phrase, "going off half
cocked," has come to mean taking action before being fully prepared.

A gun discharges when its hammer pushes the firing pin into the
primer. Because of their construction, early single-action revolvers were
likely to discharge accidentally when dropped. On some revolvers, the
firing pin is a protrusion from the hammer itself. On others, the hammer and firing pin are two separate components, and the hammer drops
onto the firing pin. Either way, the firing pin normally projects through
the breech face, resting in close proximity to the primer in the base of

How a Revolver Works

40   the cartridge. If a gun is dropped, the hammer can push the firing pin into the primer and cause the gun to discharge. One way to minimize the risk of unintentional discharge with a single-action revolver is to load a six-chamber revolver with five cartridges, and carry the gun with the empty chamber under the hammer.

Public Health Implication: Gun safety education stresses the importance of carrying a gun with the empty chamber under the hammer, and avoiding the use of the half-cocked hammer position. But these safety teachings may be ignored or forgotten. Taking these precautions is analogous to voluntarily buckling your seatbelt or choosing to wear a motorcycle helmet. From the point of view of injury prevention, it is usually more effective to design products so that individuals do not have to choose between safety and convenience with every use.

FIGURE 3.2 A FIRING PIN IN A SINGLE-ACTION REVOLVER. This is a Sturm Ruger revolver prior to modification. This single-action revolver is cocked. The firing pin can be seen protruding from the breech face ready to be struck by the hammer when the hammer is released from its position by the trigger pull. Guns of this design were subject to unintentional discharge if dropped in such a way that forces were transmitted through the uncocked hammer to the firing pin.

How a Revolver Works

All but the least expensive revolvers manufactured today are double-action revolvers. However, in the 1950s Sturm Ruger & Co. manufactured a single-action revolver, as a replica of the 1873 Colt Peacemaker, that was responsible for numerous accidental discharges.[1] In 1973, Sturm Ruger & Co. and other manufacturers introduced a gap between the hammer and the firing pin and a "safety" lever—a metal transfer bar that bridges the gap when the shooter pulls the trigger. The transfer bar is safely out of the way when the gun is cocked or uncocked. As the shooter pulls the trigger, the bar moves up and into position to transfer the energy from the falling hammer to the firing pin. However, from 1973 until the 1980s Sturm Ruger & Co. continued to sell its remaining stock without the transfer bar despite continued reports of injury from accidental discharge.[2] The technology for preventing discharge after dropping dates back to the late 1800s, but manufacturers are not required to use it.

Many modern double-action revolvers are built with a variation of another internal feature that prevents the firing pin from contacting

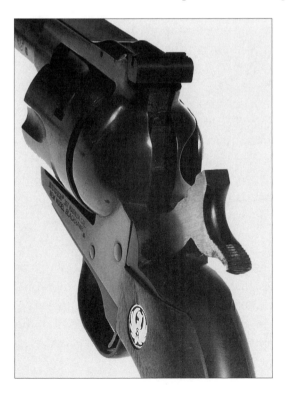

FIGURE 3.3 REVOLVER MODIFIED WITH TRANSFER BAR. A model of the revolver seen in Figure 3.2, but with a metal transfer bar. In this model there is a gap between the firing pin and the hammer so that the hammer cannot strike the firing pin if accidentally dropped. The transfer bar, which can be seen as it moves over the firing pin, moves into place to bridge the gap between the firing pin and the hammer when the trigger is pulled so that the firing pin is struck by the hammer.

How a Revolver Works

the cartridge unless the shooter squeezes the trigger. With this feature, a hammer block, the hammer flies forward when the trigger is pulled but rebounds somewhat under spring pressure, and is then prevented from moving forward again by a mechanical device that comes into play. Some manufacturers have been making revolvers with this feature since it was invented in the late nineteenth century.

Inexpensively made revolvers are often manufactured without these safety features or have safety features made from marginal materials.

Public Health Implication: The Sturm Ruger & Co. replica of the Colt 1873 Peacemaker was the subject of an important news article by journalist Eric Larson in the *Wall Street Journal* (24 June 1993). He reported on the estimated forty deaths and six hundred injuries that had resulted from unintentional discharges when the gun was dropped.[1] Some people were killed when the guns fell from wall displays. Larson pointed out that guns were unlike other consumer products in that there was no requirement for a recall of a product with a hazardous design, nor were any records kept by manufacturers and sellers to help in notifying owners of problems. No government agency has authority to monitor firearm safety or to maintain standards for their safety performance. For automobiles, on the other hand, the National Highway Traffic Safety Administration has the authority to require that manufacturers recall vehicles with hazardous designs. Sometimes the threat of a mandate to recall is enough to prompt a manufacturer to act on its own. The Dodge Minivan, for example, had an inadequate rear door latch that was associated with about twenty deaths in crashes. Before federal authorities issued a mandate, the company acted on its own to offer a new latch assembly to all owners of these vehicles.[3]

How a Revolver Is Loaded

Revolvers are commonly loaded in one of three ways. Although these loading methods all were designed in the nineteenth century, they can still be found on revolvers manufactured today. Unlike semiautomatic pistols and long arm repeaters which eject the empty case as part of the repeating action, empty cases from spent cartridges have to be removed from the revolver before new cartridges are loaded.

How a Revolver Is Loaded

SIDE-GATE. In this revolver, the cylinder is housed within a solid frame but its rear is covered on one side by a loading gate. To unload the revolver, a shooter opens the gate and manually pushes out each case with a rod that sits alongside or beneath the barrel. As each chamber is emptied, a new cartridge can be inserted. The cylinder is rotated by hand for each chamber but the cylinder stays within the frame of the revolver and the back of the cylinder is never fully exposed. This is the oldest design and is most commonly found on single-action revolvers.

BREAK-OPEN. The revolver has a hinge near the breech end. When the top catch is released, the revolver "breaks open" and the shooter folds the barrel and cylinder away from the grip. The shooter ejects all the cartridges or spent cases at once by pushing a star-shaped extractor. This revolver was more common in the U.S. in the 1920s and 1930s.

SWING-OUT CYLINDER. In this revolver the cylinder swings out from the frame at the release of a catch, exposing the rear of the entire cylinder. There is also a star-shaped extractor which is worked by pressing an extractor rod. Once the spent cases are removed in this way, all six chambers are available for reloading, and, when full, the cylinder is returned to the revolver, and the catch is reengaged.

FIGURE 3.4 A BREAK-OPEN REVOLVER. This revolver is designed to break open so the cylinder can be loaded at the breach. This design was more common in the United States during the 1920s and 1930s. This particular gun is also equipped with a grip safety.

How a Revolver Is Loaded

44   The cylinders of various models of revolvers rotate in different directions during firing. The cylinders of Colt revolvers rotate clockwise, for example, while those of Smith & Wesson revolvers rotate counterclockwise.[4]

FIGURE 3.5 A SWING-OUT CYLINDER ON A REVOLVER.
The empty chambers of the cylinder can easily be seen on this revolver where the cylinder has been swung out and is in position to be loaded.

TABLE 3.1 PRICES OF COMMON REVOLVER CARTRIDGES	
Cartridge	Retail Price per 50 Rounds[5]
.22 LR (long rifle)	$2
.32 S&W (Smith & Wesson)	$17
.357 Magnum	$25
.38 Special	$17
.44 Magnum	$20

How a Revolver Is Loaded

Why do we care about the price of guns and ammunition? In this society, price influences the availability of consumer products. If we seek to affect the widespread availability of guns and ammunition, one strategy may be to somehow increase their prices. For alcohol and tobacco this has been done with taxes—either excise taxes paid by the manufacturer or taxes imposed on the consumer at the time of sale. Young people are said to be especially sensitive to increasing the price of alcoholic beverages. Their consumption is lessened because they do not have as much disposable income as other groups. Increasing taxes on guns and ammunition has been proposed in federal legislation both as a means of decreasing the easy availability of weapons and to pay for the social costs of firearm injuries and deaths. While some argue against this because it would unduly affect the poor, finding nonlethal and affordable means of self-protection would benefit many.[6] Currently, those groups that are disadvantaged face much higher risks of homicide and unintentional death from firearms than other groups in our society.

TABLE 3.2 PRICES AND CHARACTERISTICS OF SOME COMMON REVOLVERS

Price range	Retail Price[5]	Some Models	Characteristics and Ammunition
inexpensive	$60-$80	EAA Bounty Hunter	5-inch barrel, shoots .22 LR, 6 shot, single action
	$160	North American Minirevolver	1.1-inch barrel, shoots .22 LR, 5 shot, single action
moderate	$365	Smith & Wesson Model 31 Police regulation	2-inch barrel, .32 S&W long, 6 shot, double action
	$425	Ruger GP-100	3, 4, or 6-inch barrel, .38 special, .357 Magnum, 6 shot, double action
expensive	$815–935	Colt Python	4, 6, or 8-inch barrel, .357 Magnum, .38 special, Revolver 6 shot, double action.
	$1,020	ERMA Er-777 Sporting Revolver (German import)	4 or 5.5-inch barrel, .357 Magnum, 6 shot, double action

How a Revolver Is Loaded

The two main types of pistols are derringers and semiautomatic handguns. As with much other weapon technology, semiautomatic handguns were developed to increase the rate of fire. Although the semiautomatic pistol design was pioneered around the beginning of the twentieth century, it was unreliable and expensive. Recent technological advances have made semiautomatic pistols more reliable. Increased reliability, combined with a magazine capacity that typically exceeds the number of chambers in most revolver cylinders, has recently motivated many law enforcement agencies to exchange revolvers for semiautomatic handguns. In addition, a semiautomatic pistol is smaller and thinner than a revolver that shoots the same number of similar-sized bullets.

However, because semiautomatic pistols can be mechanically more complicated than revolvers and the magazine design is critical for their reliability, poor-quality models are at higher risk of jamming or misfiring.

Overall, the number of revolvers, rifles, and shotguns manufactured in this country has been decreasing recently, while the proportion of semiautomatic pistols manufactured has been increasing. This is covered in more detail in Chapter 6.

Public Health Implication: Understanding the relationship between the kind of weapons available to the public and the firearm injury and death rates from suicide, homicide, and unintentional shootings is extremely important, but difficult to achieve with available data. Developing firearm injury reporting systems which include information on the victim and shooter, the make and model of the weapon, the ammunition used, and the circumstances surrounding the shooting would be an important step in supplying the necessary information.[7, 8] This should be coupled with information on the kinds of weapons owned by the uninjured population as well.[9]

How a Semiautomatic Pistol Works

A semiautomatic pistol is technically an autoloader. Ammunition is stored in an internal magazine, usually in the pistol grip. With each pull of the trigger the action discharges a cartridge, extracts the empty cartridge case from the chamber, ejects the case from the firearm, feeds another cartridge into the chamber from the magazine, and recocks the gun for the next shot. Some people refer to autoloaders as "automatic weapons," but the only fully automatic weapons are those that fire successive rounds with a single trigger pull. With a semiautomatic handgun, the operation of the loading mechanism is automatic, but the gun discharges only one cartridge with each pull of the trigger.

Just as with revolvers, there are single-action and double-action semiautomatic pistols. Single-action and double-action revolvers differ with respect to how the action works on every shot. By contrast, single-action and double-action semiautomatic pistols differ with respect to how the action works on the first shot only.

With a single-action semiautomatic pistol, the shooter must manually cock the handgun before pulling the trigger for the first shot. Thereafter, the discharge from each blast powers the loading mechanism and recocks the handgun for the next shot. To fire the gun, the shooter exerts the same amount of pressure each time he pulls the trigger.

With a double-action semiautomatic pistol, the first squeeze of the trigger both cocks and discharges the firearm. The shooter need not manually cock the handgun before the first shot. As with the single-action semiautomatic pistol, each discharge recocks the gun for the next shot. After the first shot, the gun operates in single-action mode for successive shots. This means that the shooter must exert more pressure on the trigger for the first shot than for successive shots.

After the shooter has finished firing, both single-action and double-action semiautomatics remain cocked. Some handguns have a decocking lever, a manually operated device that lets the shooter lower the hammer from its cocked position without having to squeeze the trigger. A third design, the double-action-only (DAO) semiautomatic pistol, eliminates the need for a decocking lever. With this type of pistol, the blast from each discharge powers the loading mechanism, but does not recock the gun for the next shot. Each pull of the trigger both cocks and discharges the weapon. The shooter exerts the same amount of pressure on the trigger for each shot, although the required pressure is greater than for the single-action semiautomatic.

How a Semiautomatic Pistol Works

Public Health Implication: Independent of their other physical characteristics such as their size, caliber, and appearance, semiautomatic pistols vary with respect to how they work. These variations can influence a shooter's ability to aim in two ways: (1) Some guns require greater trigger pressure than others, and (2) with some guns the required trigger pressure varies from shot to shot. In addition, most semiautomatics recock themselves after firing, but some do not. The way guns work may affect the way someone chooses a gun for his or her particular needs. But the lack of uniformity in the way guns work may lead to confusion among untrained shooters. Furthermore, we might view the double-action-only pistol as a "safer" handgun because it is not cocked after each shot and its trigger pull is consistent across all shots. But most DAO pistols are manufactured without external, manually operated safety devices; with no manual safeties and no decocking levers, these handguns are considered more snag resistant for concealed-carry use. Garen Wintemute describes how manufacturers promote DAO pistols in this manner, emphasizing their simple design as an advantage for those who want to "just draw and shoot."[10] Making firearm use and concealability easier may lead to an increase in deaths and injuries. Unfortunately, we do not have the necessary data systems to monitor the effects of these new designs, nor do we have the means of bringing about a change in the situation if such a study were to reveal an increase in deaths and injuries.

The blowback system, the major mechanism for powering the semiautomatic pistol's loading mechanism, was designed at the end of the nineteenth century. After each shot, a series of spring-operated mechanisms uses the energy of the recoil to move an empty cartridge case out of the chamber and a fresh cartridge into the chamber. Prior to the development of semiautomatic handguns, some autoloading systems had been developed for fully automatic weapons. However, these autoloading mechanisms were so heavy that they could only be installed on weapons fired from a support, not on small arms, and certainly not on handguns. In their quest to increase the firing rate of single-person weapons, manufacturers developed light semiautomatic mechanisms first for handguns and later for rifles. Luger, a German designer, invented a semiautomatic pistol that became famous prior to

How a Semiautomatic Pistol Works

Fully automatic rifles were subsequently developed, **49** around 1918.

To extract and eject an empty cartridge case and feed a fresh cartridge into the chamber, semiautomatic pistols use either the blowback design or one of several variations on the "locked breech" design. The major difference between these designs is in whether the barrel and the breech block remain fixed together during firing. The breech block is the rear wall of the chamber, against which the base of the cartridge rests. In most implementations of either design, the slide plays a key role. The slide is a spring-loaded piece of metal that covers the top of the gun. The force of the discharge propels the slide rearward from its resting position, and a spring returns it to its forward position.

THE BLOWBACK DESIGN. With the blowback system, the breech block is not locked to the barrel during the discharge of the cartridge. The barrel stays in place and expanding gas from the burning propellant forces the breech block rearward, creating a gap through which a spring-operated mechanism can eject the empty case. As the return spring pulls the slide forward, it powers a feeding mechanism that moves a fresh cartridge from the magazine into the chamber. Handguns designed to fire lesser powered ammunition often incorporate blowback designs.

THE LOCKED BREECH DESIGN. With this system, the breech block and the barrel are locked to each other during the discharge of the cartridge, but a mechanical device separates the barrel from the breech block after the bullet exits the barrel. The mechanism may use a series of joints with a toggle action, as with the original Luger design. Or it may use interlocking teeth on the barrel and slide, which hold them together during the first part of their rearward travel but disengage so that the slide can push the breech further rearward. There are other variations on this theme, but, in any case, the locking and unlocking mechanism is activated by the energy of the blast. As with the blowback design, the slide powers the feeding mechanism as a return spring pulls it forward. Weapons designed for more powerful ammunition use the locked breech design.

How a Semiautomatic Pistol Is Loaded

Almost all semiautomatic pistols have a removable magazine which is usually stored in the grip. To load a pistol, the shooter fills the magazine with cartridges and inserts the magazine into the pistol by sliding it into the grip. Before firing the first shot, the shooter must "charge" the weapon (pull back the slide and release it, letting the spring pull the slide forward) to cock the action and chamber the first cartridge in one motion. Energy from firing each cartridge propels the slide backwards. As it travels backward from its resting position, the slide powers the extractor, which pulls the empty case from the chamber, and the ejector, which throws the case out of the gun. As the spring pulls the slide forward again, the slide powers the feeding mechanism that moves a fresh cartridge from the magazine to the chamber.

The slide catch on a semiautomatic pistol is a small piece of metal that is attached to the side of the frame. With the slide in its normal forward position, the slide catch rests beneath the lower edge of the slide. When the slide is near its rearmost position, one end of the slide catch can be raised to fit into a notch on the slide, preventing the slide from returning to its forward position. With the slide held back, the top of the gun is open and the shooter can see into the chamber to determine whether it contains a cartridge.

With a pull of the trigger, the pistol fires a bullet, ejects the spent cartridge, chambers a fresh cartridge, and recocks the action. The shooter fires all the remaining bullets by pulling the trigger until the gun is out of ammunition. Then, the shooter reloads the gun by inserting new cartridges into the magazine or inserting a preloaded magazine.

Public Health Perspective: Some semiautomatic weapons are equipped with a safety device that does not allow the gun to be shot if the magazine has been removed, even if there is a cartridge in the chamber. Others are not equipped with this device and unintentional shootings result. The shooter may assume the pistol is unloaded since there is no magazine in it, pull the trigger, and so fires the cartridge that remains in the chamber.[11] Each year there are deaths caused by such a situation: "I didn't know the gun was loaded," is the frequent complaint.

Many semiautomatic pistols and most revolvers have exposed hammers that visibly protrude from the rear of the firearm. Other pistols have internal hammers or recessed hammers that are entirely covered by the slide or rounded off to a lower profile. Others have no hammer of

How a Semiautomatic Pistol Is Loaded

applied to these are "dropped hammer" or "hammerless" handguns.

Public Health Implication: Sometimes a gun's mechanical attributes influence a person's choice of a firearm and sometimes its cosmetic attributes influence that choice. Hammerless pistols are reported to be favored by some shooters who carry concealed weapons because the absence of an external hammer reduces the chance of the gun getting snagged on a purse, fanny pack, or seam as the shooter draws it.[10]

Larger and Larger Magazines

Small semiautomatic pistols often hold seven cartridges, one in the chamber and six in the magazine. Larger ones hold considerably more. Prior to federal legislation in 1994, pistols were commonly manufactured with magazines that held fifteen to twenty or more cartridges. Shooters could also purchase extended magazines that held thirty-two or more cartridges.

Public Health Implication: The Violent Crime Control and Law Enforcement Act of 1994, more commonly known as the Assault Weapons Ban, required that no magazines holding more than ten cartridges be manufactured for the civilian population or imported. However, it is still relatively easy to buy large-capacity magazines that were manufactured before this law was enacted.[12] As with revolvers and repeating actions, extended magazines continue the weapons development trend of moving away from single-shot weapons to multiple-shot weapons, increasing the speed with which shots can be fired. A larger magazine means greater wounding potential and more ways to inflict damage. Eleven rounds in a weapon is nearly twice the firepower of a conventional revolver.

Public Health Implication: Among the models listed in Table 3.3 is one that points to a relatively new phenomenon in semiautomatic pistol design: the use of larger caliber bullets in small, inexpensive handguns.[13] The Davis .380 is a midrange caliber gun, but it is sized similarly and priced competitively with the small caliber, .22 or .25 guns.

FIGURE 3.6 A GLOCK SEMIAUTOMATIC PISTOL IN A LOADING POSITION. The magazine can be seen in a loading position in the grip of the pistol.

TABLE 3.3 PRICES AND CHARACTERISTICS
OF SOME COMMON SEMIAUTOMATIC PISTOLS

Price Range	Retail Price[5]	Model	Characteristics and Ammunition
inexpensive	$70	Phoenix Arms Raven	2.5-inch barrel, 6-shot magazine, .25 ACP
	$98	Davis P-380	2.8-inch barrel, 6-shot magazine, .380 ACP
moderate	$462–493	Colt Government Model 380	3.25-inch barrel, 7-shot magazine, .380 ACP
expensive	$600	Glock 17 Auto	4.5-inch barrel, 10-shot magazine, 9 mm Para.
	$630	Beretta Model 92FS	4.9-inch barrel, 10-shot magazine, 9 mm Para.

Larger and Larger Magazines

FIGURE 3.7 A GLOCK SEMIAUTOMATIC PISTOL IN A COCKED POSITION. The Glock semi-automatic pistol here has the slide (the top metal piece) pulled back and the magazine loaded into its grip. Before firing the first shot, the slide is pulled back and released. This cocks the action and brings the first cartridge into the chamber. The slide also moves back with each subsequent shot and powers the devices which remove the empty cartridge case from the chamber and the gun itself. With a spring to pull it forward, the slide also powers the feeding mechanism to move the next cartridge into the chamber

TABLE 3.4 PRICES OF COMMON SEMIAUTOMATIC PISTOL CARTRIDGES

Cartridge Name	Retail Price Per 50 Rounds [5]
.22 LR	$2
.25 ACP	$18
.357 Magnum	$25
.380 ACP	$20
9 mm Para.	$24
.45 ACP	$28

Larger and Larger Magazines

As we discussed in our section on the history of small arms, the term "rifle" refers to a long arm that has a rifled bore. To quickly review, rifled barrels have spiral grooves cut into their inner surfaces. As a bullet accelerates through the rifled barrel, it grips the raised areas between the grooves, called lands, and acquires a spin around its long axis. This spin stabilizes an elongated bullet so that it flies like a well-thrown football rather than end over end.

As a gun fires a bullet, its lands and grooves cut a distinctive pattern into the bullet's surface. Forensic specialists use the spacing of the markings from the lands and grooves to determine the type of weapon from which a bullet was fired.

The bullet's tight fit in the barrel allows little or no gas to escape around the edge of the bullet. The rifle's relatively long barrel means that the bullet has a long distance over which to accelerate. A longer barrel also provides a longer time over which to impart the gyroscopic spin, making for a faster spin and hence a more stable flight. As a result, the bullet goes farther and faster. Rifles are more accurate than handguns because of their bullets' velocities and increased stability in flight. Because of their power and range, rifles are best suited to shooting targets at long distance. Civilians use them commonly in hunting large game.

Rifled bores are found not only on rifles but also on modern handguns. Rifled bores are contrasted with those of shotguns, the smoothbore long arms that we will discuss in a separate section.

How a Rifle Works

Modern rifles are either single-shot rifles, manual repeaters, or semiautomatic loaders. Single-shot rifles are loaded with a single cartridge and have to be reloaded after each shot. Manual repeating actions were developed in the last half of the nineteenth century and are still in use. Each of the three main types of manual repeaters, the lever-action, bolt-action and slide-action rifles, is named for the type of mechanism that the shooter uses to power the action. Each mechanism works slightly differently but all serve to eject the spent case and move a new cartridge into the chamber, or to let this be done manually. All three actions have an external device that moves internal springs and all can be found on modern rifles and shotguns.

LEVER-ACTION. With this type of manual repeater, the shooter powers the action by manipulating a handle or lever on the underside of the stock. From its resting position against the stock, the shooter pulls the lever down and forward toward the barrel and then pushes it back.

BOLT-ACTION. The shooter powers the action by manipulating a bolt-like mechanism on the top and to the side of the receiver. From its resting position, the shooter raises the bolt and pulls it toward him then pushes it forward and down into place again.

SLIDE OR PUMP-ACTION. The shooter powers the action by working a slide or pump on the underside of the receiver and barrel.

The long barrel of the rifle gives the weapon certain advantages. If a firearm has front and rear sights, a shooter aims the firearm by aligning the appropriate marks on the two sights with the targeted object. As a rifle's front and rear sights are relatively far apart, compared to the front and rear sights of a handgun, the increased distance makes it possible to do a better job of aiming the firearm. In combination with the rifle's inherently better accuracy, the longer sight line gives the shooter much greater control when it comes to placing a bullet on the target.

Semiautomatic and Automatic Rifles

As with pistols, the technologic imperative for long arms has been to increase the range, accuracy, and rate of fire. Increases in all three of these occurred over many hundreds of years, but increases in the rate of fire took a quantum leap forward with the development of semiautomatic and fully automatic weapons at the end of the nineteenth century. To compare the rates of fire, consider that a trained soldier with a muzzleloader could fire four rounds per minute. With a lever-action or bolt-action repeater, the rate increased to fifteen rounds per minute. Many shooters can easily fire thirty to sixty shots per minute with a semiautomatic firearm, and a fully automatic rifle can fire six hundred rounds per minute.

Both semiautomatic and automatic weapons harness part of the energy from the propellant's expanding gas to power the action. These weapons differ in the number of shots they can fire with each pull of

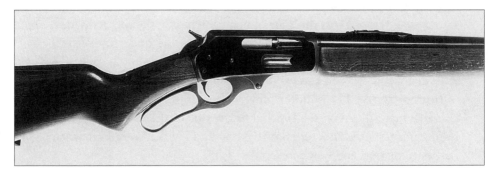

FIGURE 3.8 A LEVER-ACTION RIFLE. The lever is seen at the bottom of the rifle, surrounding the trigger and extending beneath the stock. The lever activates mechanical devices inside the rifle to eject a spent case and move a new cartridge into the firing chamber.

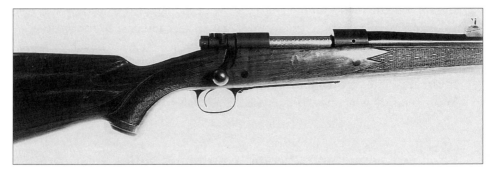

FIGURE 3.9 A BOLT-ACTION RIFLE. The bolt is the rounded knob that extends downward on the side of the rifle and is attached to the top. The bolt is raised and pulled toward the shooter, then pushed forward and down.

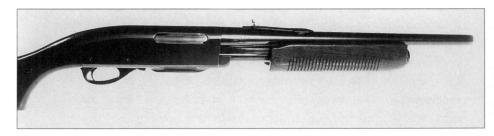

FIGURE 3.10 A SLIDE-ACTION RIFLE. The slide is the wooden piece on the bottom of the barrel that is pulled back toward the breech and returned to position.

Semiautomatic and Automatic Rifles

the trigger. A semiautomatic firearm can fire only one. Some shooters equip their semiautomatic arms with trigger accelerators, a device which "pumps" the trigger repeatedly. The practical effect is that the firearm discharges multiple cartridges in quick succession without the shooter having to execute a complete pull of the trigger for each shot. This results in a faster rate of fire than the semiautomatic arm would otherwise have.

With just one pull of the trigger, the typical fully automatic firearm discharges a cartridge, extracts and ejects the empty cartridge case, feeds another cartridge into the chamber, discharges the new cartridge and so on, over and over until the ammunition is depleted or the shooter's finger leaves the trigger. Given their extremely fast firing rates and the relatively great recoil from each shot, some automatic rifles are very difficult for the shooter to control. To compensate for this, some automatic weapons fire a three-shot burst with each trigger pull rather than an uninterrupted stream of bullets.

A machine gun is a fully automatic firearm. A submachine gun is a portable fully automatic firearm that fires pistol cartridges. Submachine guns were designed for close combat in trench warfare, although most were developed too late for World War I, the last war with trench warfare. In this century, manufacturers have developed and sold fully automatic rifles and handguns, which are considered submachine guns. Perhaps the most famous American submachine gun was the Thompson Model 1928, better known as the Tommy-gun. Mobsters made it famous during Prohibition and it was widely used in World War II. It held twenty or thirty rounds or could be fitted with drum magazines that held fifty or a hundred rounds. It also shot pistol-caliber ammunition: .45 ACP.

In the United States, the purchase of automatic weapons for civilian use has been limited since 1934, when, along with sawed-off shotguns, automatic weapons were regulated by the federal government in the 1934 National Firearms Act as "gangster weapons." Retail customers were required to pay a transfer tax and to give law enforcement agents a justification for the purchase. In 1986, legislation was passed to prohibit the production and sale of automatic weapons to civilians.

Public Health Implication: Increasing the rate of fire increases the wounding potential of the weapon, either by increasing the number of shots that hit the target or by increasing the number of targets

Semiautomatic and Automatic Rifles

that can be hit within the same time period. While automatic weapons have been more difficult for civilians to obtain than other weapons since the mid 1930s and their production for the civilian population has been prohibited since 1986, semiautomatic weapons can be converted to automatic fire with simple devices added to the gun's action. These devices may be difficult for law enforcement officials to detect. Each year five hundred to a thousand of these converted weapons are brought to the attention of the Bureau of Alcohol, Tobacco, and Firearms (ATF) by law enforcement agencies. The policies which originally led to stricter controls over automatic weapons have not kept pace with technology that allows for this type of conversion.

Shotguns

Shotguns are smooth-bore weapons that fire cartridges filled with shot—multiple small pellets. Because the shot is widely dispersed it does not travel far, so the shotgun is a short-range weapon used for fast-moving targets, like fowl or small mammals, within a hundred and

TABLE 3.5 PRICES AND CHARACTERISTICS OF SOME COMMON RIFLES

Price Range	Retail Price[5]	Some Models	Characteristics
inexpensive	$175	Chipmunk	.22 rimfire, single shot
moderate	$600	Winchester 70	centerfire, bolt action
expensive	$1,300	Weatherby Mark V Deluxe	centerfire, bolt action

TABLE 3.6 PRICES OF COMMON RIFLE CARTRIDGES

Cartridge Name	Retail Price per 50 Rounds[5]
.22	$2
.22 Remington	$14
.30-06	$17
.30-30	$18
7 mm Magnum	$21

Shotguns

fifty feet. At short range it inflicts a tremendous amount of tissue damage. At longer range the dispersion of the shot increases the chances that some part of the fast moving target will be hit. The shotgun's ammunition and smooth bore are the physical characteristics that distinguish it from the rifle, the other type of long arm.

The parts of a shotgun cartridge are a shell, which is usually made out of plastic or paper, with a metal cap on the base; percussion primer, as with other modern cartridges; powder, for generating the explosive gases; a felt wad, or a plastic cup, which separates the powder and the shot to facilitate the smooth acceleration of the whole load of shot; and a load of shot. Shot are little pellets made of drop lead (lead with antimony and/or arsenic). A single shotgun shell can hold hundreds of pellets.

Some shotgun shells contain a single-rifled "slug" instead of the more common load of shot. Some urban and suburban communities do not allow use of rifles during hunting season because of concern about stray bullets in which case a shooter might use a shotgun with a deer slug. Rifled slugs may be constructed entirely of lead and "finned" or grooved around their outside diameter, or they may have fiber or plastic wads attached to the base. Because a slug acquires no gyroscopic spin from the shotgun's smooth bore, its behavior in the air is not nearly as efficient as that of a bullet. For the rest of this discussion, we concentrate on the more traditional loads of shot.

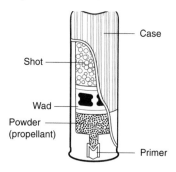

FIGURE 3.11 THE PARTS OF A SHOT-GUN CARTRIDGE. The load of shot that is carried by the shell can vary from small birdshot to large buckshot.

Shot is made in a range of sizes. The diameter of the shot decreases as the amount per cartridge increases. Buck shot ranges from No. 4 Buck at .24 inches in diameter and three hundred and forty to the pound, to No. 00 at .32 inches and a hundred and thirty to the pound. Buck shot, with its larger pellets, is used for large animals; bird shot, with smaller pellets, is used for fowl and small game.

The measure of the size of the shell is called a gauge. Common sizes are 10, 12, 16, 20, 28, and 410. A 10-gauge shotgun is the largest common one and has significant recoil.

60   Shotguns come with various ways to adjust the choke, which is what affects the dispersion of the shot after it leaves the muzzle and is adjusted depending on the range of the target. The amount of choke determines how dense or loose the shot pattern will be and is described in terms of its effect on the shot pattern at a distance of forty yards. An open-choked barrel produces wider dispersion, and a tighter-choked barrel reduces the dispersion. A shooter would use full choke for a target at long range, so that the pellets would be at an optimal pattern at about thirty to fifty yards. A shotgun with less choke would disperse the pellets earlier for a closer target at about twenty to thirty yards.

How a Shotgun Works

Modern shotguns have six basic action types. Repeating actions are essentially the same as for rifles and are described in that section.

SINGLE-SHOT, BREAK-TOP. This shotgun holds one shot and the shooter loads it after "breaking" it open at its hinged point beneath the breech end of the barrel.

BOLT-ACTION. This is a manual repeater like the bolt-action repeating rifle where a shooter works the action by moving a bolt back and forth.

SLIDE OR PUMP-ACTION. Also a manual repeater where the shooter works the action by moving a slide on the underside of the barrel.

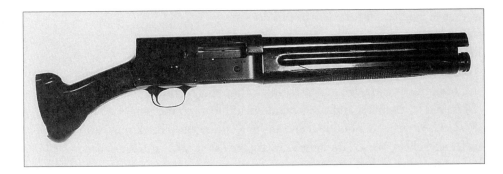

FIGURE 3.12 A SAWED-OFF SHOTGUN. The barrel of this shotgun has literally been sawed off to make the weapon easier to conceal. Sawed-off shotguns have been illegal since the 1934 National Firearms Act.

How a Shotgun Works

one-shot barrels, one next to the other. On a double-barreled shotgun the two barrels usually have different degrees of choke. The shooter fires each barrel separately. Like the single-shot shotgun, this firearm is "broken open" at the breech for loading.

OVER-AND-UNDER DOUBLE-BARRELED SHOTGUN. This is like the side-by-side, but the two barrels are stacked vertically.

AUTOLOADER. This is a repeating shotgun that works on the same principle as an autoloading or semiautomatic rifle.

One way to understand shotguns is to think of them as being exactly what rifles and handguns are not. Rifles and handguns allow relatively fine control of a single projectile over a relatively long distance. Shotguns are relatively short-range tools that throw several hundred tiny pellets in a pattern that spreads out as the range increases. Compared to a rifle or handgun, a shotgun is a much more effective tool for hitting a moving target. In shooting at a moving target, the shooter

TABLE 3.7 PRICES AND CHARACTERISTICS OF SOME COMMON SHOTGUNS

Price Range	*Retail Price*[5]	*Some Models*	*Characteristics and Ammunition*
inexpensive	$230–293	Maverick Model 88	Pump action, 12 gauge
moderate	$340	Winchester Model 1300	Pump action, 12 and 20 gauge, 5 shot
expensive	$1,400	Beretta 686 Onyx	Over/under, double barreled, 12, 20, 28 gauge

TABLE 3.8 PRICES OF COMMON SHOTGUN AMMUNITION

Shell	*Retail Price Per Box of 25*[5]
12 gauge 3" mag	$10
20 gauge 3" mag	$15
28 gauge 2–3/4" mag	$12
410 Bore 3" inch mag	$9

How a Shotgun Works

moves his upper body in the same arc as the target, pointing slightly ahead of it to allow for the distance the target will travel between the time the trigger is pulled and the time the shot arrives at the target. In many hunting situations the shooter is more likely to "point" the shotgun rather than "aim" it, as is required for effective use of a hand-gun or rifle.

Sawed-off shotguns have had the barrel literally sawed off, usually where the front of the stock ends. The intent in sawing off the barrel is to make the gun small enough to be easily concealed. Any kind of shotgun can be made into a sawed-off shotgun. Sawed-off shotguns were made illegal as "gangster weapons" by the 1934 National Firearms Act which specified a minimum barrel length of eighteen inches for shotguns and sixteen inches for rifles.

How a Shotgun Works

4

Comparing Firearms

The evolution of small arms is a story of increases in their velocity, range, accuracy, and firing rate, of the development of projectiles that produce more extensive wounds, and of the development of safety features to reduce the risk of unintentional injury to the shooter. All of these issues are also important in a comparison of contemporary firearms. Sometimes it is useful to approach these issues by comparing the physical characteristics of firearms. Sometimes it is more useful to approach them by comparing functional characteristics, that is, the effects that result from practical combinations of the physical characteristics. In this chapter we combine both approaches to describe how firearms differ. We concentrate on differences that may have some public health importance.

Magazine Capacity

How many cartridges can a magazine hold? While most revolvers hold six cartridges in their cylinders, semiautomatic pistols with standard-sized removable magazines have been manufactured to hold seventeen, nineteen, or more cartridges. Until federal legislation in 1994, many manufacturers also made extended magazines that held thirty-two cartridges. With a larger magazine capacity, a gun can fire more bullets before the shooter must reload. As larger magazines became more common, trauma physicians documented an increase in the number of victims with multiple wounds.[1] Each wound is its own threat to the victim's well-being. More wounds mean more threats. Although magazines with a capacity greater than ten rounds now cannot legally be manufactured or imported for the civilian market, many of those manufactured before the 1994 law are still available.[2]

Barrel Length

For pistols and revolvers, barrel length is an important physical characteristic. It is a common measure of the firearm's size and it correlates with ease of concealability. Practically speaking, barrel length affects the firearm's accuracy and muzzle velocity and influences whether it will be used for hunting, target shooting, or a nonsporting purpose.

A revolver's barrel length can be measured by examining the weapon's exterior, measuring from the cylinder to the muzzle end. With a semi-automatic pistol, however, the barrel is typically covered by the slide so the barrel length cannot be accurately measured by visual inspection. Although a gun's overall size can be visually assessed and measured from the exterior, the fully assembled semiautomatic pistol's barrel length can be accurately measured only on the inside of the barrel. A common way to do this is to insert a stick or rod at the muzzle and push it back to the breech of the unloaded gun.

CONCEALABILITY. A gun with a shorter barrel can be smaller overall and is more easily concealed.

VELOCITY. A firearm with a longer barrel accelerates a bullet over a greater distance and, therefore, for a longer period of time than one with a short barrel. Given identical bullets fired from guns with two different barrel lengths and an optimal amount of propellant for each barrel, the bullet fired from the gun with the longer barrel has a greater velocity as it leaves the muzzle.

ACCURACY. Accuracy is a measure of how well a firearm can place a bullet at its "point of aim," independent of the skill of the shooter. A gun's front and rear sights define a line through space and the point where that line intersects the target is called the firearm's point of aim. The "point of impact" is where the bullet actually meets the target. An accurate firearm is one whose point of impact is relatively close to its point of aim.

Like rifles, handguns have rifled bores, which gives a gyroscopic spin to the bullet thus stabilizing its flight after it leaves the barrel. A firearm with a longer barrel has more time to impart a faster spin to the bullet. The combination of the bullet's increased velocity and greater stability in flight makes the firearm more accurate over a longer distance. The corollary to the increase in accuracy and velocity is that the firearm's range increases also.

Most handguns for target shooting have barrel lengths of six inches or longer. Given a target at close range, a bullet from a handgun with a barrel length of less than four inches will probably strike some part of the target. However, a handgun with a barrel less than four inches long

cannot reliably place a bullet at its point of aim if the distance between
the gun and the target is more than several yards.

Public Health Implication: The role of concealed weapons is still being debated in this country. Traditionally, cheap, short-barreled handguns have been considered weapons that were easily obtained, easily concealed, and used in a disproportionate number of crimes and homicides.[3, 4] Carrying concealed weapons without a permit has been illegal in most jurisdictions, but many states are now either passing or considering laws that make obtaining a permit much easier.

If weapons may be concealed, law enforcement personnel can't know, and are effectively not allowed to find out, who is carrying a weapon. Thus, it is easier for a person who intends to do damage to be in public with a weapon, since the weapon is concealed. Also, if a gun may be carried into the public realm, it is at hand—for impulsive or other actions. Proponents of laws that allow concealment believe that granting permits to carriers of concealed weapons screens out those with no legitimate use for the weapon. Longer barreled handguns are harder to conceal in clothing and therefore may be less likely to be carried into high-risk situations like bars or public events. As with most policy decisions about firearms, the current discussion on concealed weapons is being debated with very little documented evidence about outcomes. There is evidence, however, that "concealed carry laws" are associated with an increase in firearm homicides.[5]

It should be noted that the discussions about concealed carry laws do not include whether to limit the kinds of weapons. It might be worth while to allow only those that can pass a drop test (e.g., they can be dropped without going off) or those that are "personalized" and can be fired only by their owners. An injury reporting system and information on weapons possessed in the population being studied would go a long way toward answering questions about the risks involved in carrying concealed weapons.

Pistols with overall lengths of less than six inches and revolvers with barrel lengths of less than three inches are banned from import into the United States by the Gun Control Act of 1968, but have been widely manufactured in the U.S. since that time. Although their manu-

Barrel Length

facture had not previously been prohibited, domestic production boomed in the wake of the import ban (see Chapter 6).

Muzzle Velocity, Kinetic Energy, and Relative Stopping Power

There are no perfect measures of the effect a bullet can produce but there are a variety of measures that attempt to describe a bullet's potential to inflict damage. Muzzle velocity, kinetic energy, and relative stopping power are three such measures. Muzzle velocity is the bullet's speed as it exits the muzzle of a gun and is measured in meters per second or feet per second. A measurement of the bullet's kinetic energy takes into account both its mass and its muzzle velocity. Kinetic energy (KE) is calculated as one-half the mass times the square of the velocity and is measured in foot-pounds in the English system and Joules in the metric system.

Kinetic energy is important because a bullet dissipates energy in the target it strikes. The greater its energy before the impact, the more energy it can dissipate in the target. If the target is human tissue, this influences the extent of tissue damage and therefore the severity of a gunshot wound.

Muzzle velocity is important for several reasons. First, the velocity is an important determinant of the bullet's kinetic energy. Second, muzzle velocity varies greatly between firearms—from approximately eight hundred feet per second for some small-caliber handguns to upwards of twenty-nine hundred feet per second for some hunting rifles. Third, muzzle velocity is easier to measure than kinetic energy. It is also sometimes easier to grasp as a concept. People who are interested in firearms sometimes speak of their power or effectiveness, but neither of these terms has a precise meaning. We use them when trying to communicate something intuitive about a firearm's ability to inflict damage. The amount of damage a firearm can do in any given situation is a function of many factors, some related to the firearm itself and some not. In summary, although muzzle velocity and kinetic energy do not directly correlate with wound severity, they are quantities that can be measured precisely and they can serve as a useful starting point for describing a firearm's wounding potential.

Relative stopping power is a term that is sometimes mistakenly used to indicate the likelihood that a bullet can "stop an assailant in his tracks." However, no bullet can be counted on to stop an onrushing assailant in his tracks. Wounds to most anatomic sites do not result in the human body's instantaneous shutdown. Relative stopping power, or RSP, differs from KE in that it describes a bullet's potential to do damage not only in terms of its mass and velocity but also in terms of its shape and cross-sectional surface area. RSP is a standard ballistics measure and was first proposed in 1920 and last modified in 1935.[6] RSP is not the only measure of a bullet or firearm's potential to inflict damage, but its use is relatively common.

Relative stopping power is a unitless quantity, calculated as: RSP = p x A x F where p is the bullet's linear momentum (mass times velocity), A is the bullet's cross-sectional surface area and F is a constant that corresponds to the shape and construction of the bullet. Given semi-jacketed and fully jacketed bullets with equal momentum and cross-sectional surface area, the RSP is greater for the blunt semi-jacketed bullet than for streamlined and fully jacketed bullets because F is larger.

The physical characteristics of firearms and ammunition that influence KE and RSP include the barrel length of the weapon, the amount and chemical makeup of the propellant in the cartridge, and the mass, diameter, design, and construction of the projectile. The table following shows that handguns and their cartridges have the lowest muzzle velocities and KEs, while rifles have considerably greater muzzle velocities and KEs. Chapter 5, Injuries from Firearms, further discusses projectile and gun characteristics and their relation to wounding potential.

Public Health Implications: Because injury is caused by a transfer of energy that the body cannot dissipate without damage to tissue, measures of the energy of various weapons and ammunition are essential for comparison and for setting standards. These measures are currently used in hunting regulations. For example, in some states it is not legal to hunt deer with ammunition that, when discharged, produces projectiles with less than twelve hundred foot-pounds of energy. Rifles with less force than this increase the probability of a deer being wounded and having a prolonged death, which is thought to be less humane. Researchers have measured the maximum amount of energy that the human body can dissipate at various anatomic sites without damage. Such information is commonly used to set manufac-

Relative Stopping Power

turing standards for consumer products. For example, to reduce the likelihood of head injury in the event of a car crash, the regulatory standards for automobile occupant compartments were based on measurements of how much energy the human head could dissipate without damage. We do not have this regulatory structure for firearms, but we do have it for other consumer products.

Inexpensive revolvers and pistols have traditionally been manufactured in .22 and .25 caliber models. Even though these are small guns with small bullets, they are still lethal weapons. Increasingly, however, larger caliber models are being manufactured and sold.[3, 7] Nine mm pistols have ten times the stopping power of .25 caliber pistols, and, although stopping power is not a direct measure of wounding potential, a bullet's kinetic energy determines the maximum amount of energy it can transfer to the body of the shooting victim. Calibers above .50 cannot be sold to the civilian population. One manufacturer, though, is marketing a .50 caliber handgun and stresses that its stopping power is more than seventy times that of a

TABLE 4.1 MUZZLE VELOCITY AND KINETIC ENERGY OF COMMON CARTRIDGES[8]

Cartridge Caliber	Muzzle Velocity (feet per second)	Kinetic Energy (foot-pounds)
Typical Handgun	**820–1,300**	**65–1,000**
.22 LR	1,080	93
.25	815	66
.32	970	125
.380	1,000	166
9 mm	1,355	189
.357 Magnum	1,450	583
.45 auto	917	421
.44 Magnum	1,610	1,045
Typical Rifle	**2,000–3,300**	**1,000–5,000**
.22 Hornet	2,690	723
.243 Winchester	3,350	1,993
.30-30 Winchester	2,390	1,902
.30-06 Springfield	2,910	2,820
.460 Weatherby Magnum	2,700	8,092
Shotgun 12 gauge	**1,330**	**2,145**

Relative Stopping Power

TABLE 4.2 RELATIVE STOPPING POWER OF COMMON HANDGUN CARTRIDGES   **69**

Common Pistol Cartridges	Relative Stopping Power[7]
.22 LR	5
.25 ACP	4
.32 ACP	13
.380 ACP	27
9 mm	58
.50	383

small caliber weapon.[7] With adequate data, as has been done with motor vehicle crashes, it is possible to use sophisticated statistical analyses to estimate the contribution made by different factors such as caliber and ammunition type in outcomes of injury and death.

Trigger Pull

Trigger pull refers to the amount of pressure the shooter's finger must exert to pull a trigger. For example, the amount of pressure necessary to fire a double-action revolver is twelve to fifteen pounds, while for a single-action revolver the amount of trigger pull may vary from less than a pound to as much as for a double-action revolver.

A firearm's trigger pull, or trigger pressure, can adversely affect the shooter's ability to aim, as the squeezing of a heavy trigger may cause the shooter to move the gun off target. Some dueling pistols were made with triggers that required very little pressure in order to permit the faster shooter to squeeze off the first shot with better aim. In contemporary English we still refer to a volatile person as someone who has a "hair trigger," as these triggers came to be called.

Public Health Implication: It is possible to create a trigger with a pull that is higher than a typical child could exert. This would be comparable to the childproof caps for prescription medicine and other household substances that were designed to be "significantly difficult" for children under the age of five to open. Childhood deaths from poisoning have decreased substantially since 1970 when the law for such caps was enacted.

A group of pediatricians recently compared the trigger pull of commercially available handguns with the ability of small children to

Trigger Pull

exert the necessary strength with one or two fingers.[9] The results
suggest that significant modifications in trigger pull would have to
be made. More than 90 percent of the commercial handguns they
tested had a trigger pull strength of less than ten pounds. While
only 25 percent of three to four year olds could exert this amount of
pressure with two fingers, 70 percent of five to six year olds, and 90
percent of seven to eight year olds were able to do so. The ten-
pound finger strength was chosen for study because 95 percent of
adult women are able to exert at least this much pressure with one
finger. The authors of the study concluded that increasing the trigger
pull to protect children would make the weapons difficult for some
adult women to use and that the firearms industry would be unwill-
ing to adopt this approach.[9] It appears that a practical childproof
firearm cannot be achieved just by increasing the trigger pull. But
combining trigger pull with some other mechanism might help
childproof the firearm.

Safety Devices

A safety device, or "safety" as it is commonly called, is a firearm feature that is intended to prevent or reduce the risk of an unintentional
discharge. Safeties were developed to prevent firearms from going off
when dropped or during handling. Unintentional discharge was a
problem with some early firearms because of their primitive ignition
mechanisms and the volatility of the black powder. For example, during the firing of black powder revolvers it was not uncommon for the
blast from a detonating cartridge to spark the charge in the next
chamber in line, detonating the second cartridge as well. With other
firearms, their mechanical design presented an increased risk of unintentional discharge. For example, some single-action revolvers were
particularly susceptible to going off when dropped because nothing
prevented a slight movement of the hammer from pushing the firing
pin into a cartridge's primer.

Over the years the risk of unintentional discharge has been reduced
considerably, in part because of advances in ammunition technology
and in part because of changes in firearm design. Modern smokeless
gunpowder is less volatile than black powder, and firearm ignition
mechanisms improved greatly between 1400 and 1800. But uninten-

Safety Devices

tional discharge is still an issue, and some firearms present a greater risk of unintentional discharge than others.

To reduce the risk of unintentional discharge, a modern firearm may have one of a variety of safety devices. These generally fall into three categories. First are the mechanical features that a user may manually engage or disengage to control the firearm's ability to discharge. Second are the features that control the firearm's discharge mechanism, but are not manually operated by the shooter. Third are the features that do not directly affect the mechanical operation of the firearm, but provide a visual cue to help the shooter make intelligent decisions about handling the firearm.

Perhaps the most familiar safety devices are those that the shooter operates manually. The most common of these is a two-position switch on the side of a pistol that locks the action when the switch is in the "safe" position. This switch is sometimes called a thumb safety. On some handguns, the action is locked when the switch is in the "up" position, and on others it is locked when the switch is in the "down" position. The manufacture of handguns is not subject to standards that regulate this, and manufacturers do not have a voluntary standard for which position is safe.

Public Health Implication: Without standardized safeties, it is very difficult for an individual to use different guns without risking an accidental discharge. If all guns had standard safety devices, this potentially would reduce injuries and deaths from mishandling.

A grip safety is another kind of manually operated device. A grip safety is a spring-loaded lever that protrudes from the rear of the grip on some handguns. (See Figure 3.4) When a shooter holds the gun properly, the palm of the shooter's hand depresses the lever. A firearm with a grip safety can only be discharged if the lever is depressed. The grip safety is like the "deadman's grip" found on some lawn mowers that keeps the blades from spinning unless the user's hands grasp the handle securely. The history of the gun's grip safety as a child safety device is described in Chapter 8.

Devices that the user does not manually control are also important and sometimes more subtle. The great advantage of these devices is that they reduce the risk of unintentional discharge, but do not depend on the user taking a specific action or making a decision. One such device is called a magazine safety. This device prevents the gun from

Safety Devices

discharging when the magazine is removed even if there is a cartridge in the chamber. With a semiautomatic pistol, a shooter prepares to fire by inserting the magazine into the grip and racking the slide to feed the first cartridge from the magazine into the chamber. If the shooter removes the magazine, the chambered cartridge stays in the gun. Unless the gun has a magazine safety, the shooter can fire the gun even though the magazine has been removed.

Devices that affect the firearm's ability to discharge may be divided into two categories. Positive safety devices are those that, when activated, enable the discharge. With a positive safety device the gun remains disabled until the user takes a specific action to engage the device. The grip safety is an example of a positive safety device. Negative safety devices are those that, when activated, disable the discharge. With a negative safety device, the gun remains enabled until the safety device is engaged. The magazine safety is an example of a negative safety device.

The third category of safety features are those that do not affect the firearm's ability to discharge but that provide a visual cue instead. One

FIGURE 4.1 A LOADED-CHAMBER INDICATOR. The loaded-chamber indicator on this Glock is the protrusion at the upper right, above the cocked hammer.

Safety Devices

such device is a loaded-chamber indicator which shows whether the chamber contains a cartridge. (Figure 4.1) Loaded-chamber indicators are often very discreetly visible and differ widely as to their appearance among firearms. A loaded-chamber indicator is useful if the shooter is aware of its presence. This may not be the case for someone who is not familiar with a particular gun.

Public Health Implication: There are very few safety standards, or standards of any kind, for domestically manufactured firearms, and manufacturers are under no obligation to make guns that have safety features. There are gun safety standards—minimum physical criteria—for imported handguns. By contrast, there are many safety standards for almost all other domestic and imported consumer products, including toy guns.

Technology is not a barrier to establishing safety standards for domestically manufactured guns. Manufacturers have developed many safety devices.

Often, with safety devices and other injury control measures, the technology is available but not uniformly included on all models by all manufacturers. Automobile air bags are a prime example of this. With motor vehicles, many advances in motor vehicle design that reduced injuries came when the federal government mandated federal motor vehicle safety standards. These required that passenger cars meet certain design or performance standards, such as including seat belts, or installing windshields that crack but do not shatter and, therefore, prevent passengers from being ejected.

Special Topics

Saturday Night Specials

"Saturday Night Special" is a term describing an inexpensive, easily concealed handgun of poor quality. Though the term may have originated in the early 1900s, it was reportedly popularized in Detroit in the late 1960s, though weapons of this sort have been available since Henry Deringer invented his pocket pistol. Through the years, different kinds of weapons have been considered Saturday Night Specials. In

1968, after the assassinations of Martin Luther King, Jr. and Robert Kennedy, the Gun Control Act was written to address the issue of Saturday Night Specials. At that time, many inexpensive handguns were being imported into the United States from Brazil, Italy, Spain, and Germany. Domestically produced weapons may have been as small, but were of a higher quality. This 1968 act set minimum standards for weapons imported into the United States, establishing criteria for handgun size and the quality of design and manufacture.

Minimum standards for revolvers include: a safety feature that reduces the risk of the gun going off when dropped, a minimum overall length of 4.5 inches, and a minimum barrel length of 3 inches. Beyond that, a gun cannot be imported unless an analysis of its features yields a minimum number of points on a factoring scale. Points are awarded for: barrel length, with more points added as length increases; whether the frame was made of steel or a high-test steel alloy; the weapon weight; higher caliber; and target sights. Minimum requirements for pistols include: a positive manual safety device, an overall length of six inches and an overall height of four inches. As with revolvers, points are awarded for increased barrel length, steel or high-test steel alloy construction, increased weight, larger caliber, a variety of safety features, and other miscellaneous equipment. (See Appendix 1 for the text of the Factoring Criteria Form.)

The purpose of the Factoring Criteria was to identify weapons designed and manufactured for "sporting" purposes such as target shooting and hunting weapons and to disallow the import of weapons which did not meet the criteria set for sporting purposes. Short-barreled handguns have limited accuracy beyond a range of several yards, which makes them not particularly useful for sporting purposes.

As the law was originally written in 1968, the Factoring Criteria were applied only to weapons imported into the United States. Guns manufactured domestically did not fall under the law, so an existing domestic industry grew tremendously in the wake of the legislation.[10] Until 1986, guns could also be assembled domestically from imported parts. California firearm manufacturing companies that originally took advantage of the exception now produce more than a third of all handguns manufactured in the United States (34 percent in 1992).[6] These companies (Davis Industries, Lorcin Engineering, Phoenix Arms, Bryco Arms, and Sundance Industries), owned and managed by one extended family, produce what Garen Wintemute, author of *Ring of Fire*, termed "modern Saturday Night Specials."[3] This modern Saturday Night Special is a semiautomatic pistol, increasingly a .380 ACP. According to Wintemute, these companies manufacture more than 80 percent of all the .25 caliber, .32 ACP, and .380 caliber pistols. They are expanding their product line to include 9 mm pistols as well.[3]

Public Health Implication: The increase in production of cheap high-caliber pistols is likely to result in an increase in deaths and injuries from firearms. The relative stopping power, as described above, for 9 mm pistols is more than ten times that of .25 caliber ones. We do not know the case fatality rate (ratio of deaths to inflicted injuries) for injuries inflicted with .25 caliber pistols versus 9 mm pistols; theoretically for the 9 mm the case fatality rate would be higher. Because this particular group of manufacturers produces such cheap weapons, we can assume their 9 mm weapons will be easy to purchase as well.[3] For other public health hazards, such as alcohol and tobacco, price has been shown to affect availability: the cheaper the product, the more available it is to purchase and to use. In particular, the product becomes more accessible to children and teenagers. We make an assumption that this is true for firearms as well but, as with many other important issues, this has not been well documented.

As with earlier Saturday Night Specials, the guns produced by the California companies are of poor quality. They are made not of steel, but with metal so soft (zinc) that it reportedly can be shaved with a knife.[3] The practical effect of this is that the serial number can be removed easily, making it more difficult for law enforcement agents to trace the transfer of weapons from one owner to another. Literature on firearm performance documents the unreliability of these guns: failure to feed cartridges into the chamber, jamming produced by one cartridge overriding another during the firing and loading sequence, etc.[3]

Public Health Implication: In *Ring of Fire*, Wintemute points out that even gun periodicals suggest that these weapons are not reliable enough for self-defense.[3] Since they are not accurate enough for sporting purposes, he wonders whether they have any legitimate use. The Maryland Handgun Roster agrees.[3] Established by a unique state law that forbids the manufacture, sale, or possession of Saturday Night Specials as specified by a diverse board of law enforcement agents, other public officials, firearms experts, and citizens, the roster of handguns "banned in Maryland" includes a long list of those manufactured by these California companies.[3] Unfortunately, there is no similar national legislation that slows their production or decreases their role in the domestic industry.

Assault Weapons

To the military, an assault weapon is a portable automatic weapon whose cartridges are bigger than pistol ammunition but smaller than rifle ammunition. Some are "select-fire," meaning they can be switched from semi to fully automatic. In other contexts, an assault weapon is a semiautomatic version of a fully automatic or select-fire military weapon. The category is sometimes expanded to include any semiautomatic firearm that can be converted to automatic fire with relative ease and that, because of its design and relatively low quality workmanship, does not have a legitimate sporting use.

For the purposes of the Violent Crime Control and Law Enforcement Act of 1994, more commonly known as the Assault Weapon Ban, an assault weapon is a semiautomatic handgun, rifle, or shotgun with physical characteristics as follows:

A semiautomatic rifle with a detachable magazine and at least two of the following:
A folding or telescoping stock which folds out of the way to increase concealability;

A pistol grip protruding from the frame that allows the shooter to use one hand to hold the rifle like a handgun;

A bayonet mount to which a bayonet can be easily attached;

A flash suppressor that dissipates the gases that emerge from the muzzle after discharge, to decrease the weapon's detectability during discharge in the dark (or, a threaded barrel designed to accommodate a flash suppressor or other device); and

A grenade launcher.

Assault Weapons

A magazine that attaches to the pistol at a place other than inside the grip;

A threaded barrel capable of accommodating a barrel extender, flash suppressor, forward handgrip, or silencer;

A barrel shroud, a vented metal covering the barrel, that allows the shooter to hold the front of the gun where the barrel would otherwise be too hot to touch;

A weight of more than fifty ounces when unloaded; and

A design like that of an automatic firearm except for its semi-automatic capability.

A semiautomatic shotgun that has at least two of the following:

A folding or telescoping stock;

A pistol grip;

A fixed magazine with a capacity greater than five rounds; and

A detachable magazine.

The 1994 legislation also banned the manufacture and sale of any magazine with a capacity in excess of ten rounds.

Since the federal legislation, these guns cannot be imported or manufactured for the civilian market in the United States. Any weapons with these characteristics manufactured prior to the ban can still be legally sold. (See Figures 8.2 and 8.3 for examples of weapons designed after the ban featuring designs that circumvent the purpose of the law while narrowly meeting its requirements.)

Public Health Implication: Some of these physical characteristics of assault weapons, such as the bayonet mount, do not affect the mechanical operation of the firearm. They are not likely to affect the type of use or outcomes of these weapons that the legislation was trying to prevent—notorious attacks on school children in school yards or on people in public settings like restaurants. The restriction on large magazine capacity is, however, directly related to reducing the likelihood of large numbers of people being shot. Generally, the production of military weapons for the civilian population is a common trend for manufacturers who may already have the design and process developed under military contract but now want to find another market for their products.

Serial Numbers

Each gun legally manufactured in the United States since 1968 has a serial number, usually including its year of manufacture. Manufacturers are required to record the serial numbers and dispositions of the firearms they sell to wholesalers, and wholesalers are required to record the same information when they pass firearms along to retailers.

When the gun is purchased, the retailer records the serial number on Federal Form 4473 along with the purchaser's name and address and a certification that the purchaser is not in any of the categories of people proscribed from purchasing guns, such as felons. These forms are not centrally filed nor computerized, but are available for review by ATF agents who may request them during gun traces. (The text of Form 4473 is reprinted in Appendix 2.)

While the trace is a cumbersome process, the serial number record makes it possible to identify a firearm's original place of legal purchase and its history of transfer from one legal owner to another. Serial numbers are sometimes eradicated from weapons to make them untraceable. This illegal eradication is made easier if the gun is of soft metal as is the case with some Saturday Night Specials. The role of the ATF and the legal purchase of firearms is described in Chapter 6.

Public Health Implications: The serial number of the gun, coupled with the manufacturer's identity, is probably the easiest way to record substantial information about its make and model. An analogy is the vehicle identification number or VIN of a motor vehicle. VINs are used by manufacturers, dealers, and researchers to investigate a vehicle's performance over time and to examine the relationships between vehicle characteristics and injury outcomes in crashes. VINs can be decoded to identify the make, model, year of a car, and whether it is equipped with specific features such as airbags. It is easy to record and analyze with computers. Theoretically, serial numbers of firearms could be similarly used.

Serial Numbers

Soft body armor is the technical term for the garment worn by law enforcement personnel for protection against ballistic threats. The term "bullet-proof vest" is discouraged because there is no such thing as a vest that is entirely bullet proof. Instead, vests are manufactured to a variety of standards with the most comfortable providing the least resistance. Modern body armor made from Kevlar (or aramid, the generic name) began to be developed around 1974.[11] Aramid is a highly resistant and flexible plastic that was developed for use in automobile tires. Type 1 is effective against .38 special ammunition with a maximum velocity of 850 ft/s and .22 LR ammunition with a maximum velocity of 1050 ft/s.[11] The National Institute of Justice, which sets the standards, suggests that law enforcement agents wear protection that matches the caliber of their own weapons, as research findings indicate that among law enforcement officers who get killed on the job, 21 percent are shot with their own guns.[11, 12]

Some models provide chest protection only, some have front and back panels, and others wrap around and provide side protection as well. As more protection is required, as is for rifle bullets, the armor is made tougher by inserting rigid plastic or ceramic plates into panels. Typically, Type III and IV protection are worn by special tactical units facing threats from a hidden rifle, while other models protect against handgun shots. (Table 4.3)

Early in their history, guns made obsolete the suits of armor worn by knights. Now we see a return of full body armor for protecting law enforcement agents. Body protection can also be purchased by civilians.

Public Health Implication: This form of injury prevention, protective devices for a vulnerable body part, is a common one. Soft body armor is analogous to motorcycle helmets and bicycle helmets. And like these, it will only work if the individual uses it and it only protects the part of the body covered. For law enforcement agents, body armor is often too uncomfortable to wear full time. Furthermore, the head remains uncovered.

Body Armor

Some of the emerging technologies that might affect firearm deaths and injuries involve new kinds of ammunition that have been developed, but are not yet widely used. These include:

.50 CALIBER HANDGUNS AND AMMUNITION. Civilians may not legally purchase firearms or ammunition whose caliber is greater than one-half inch. At this upper limit, however, the .50 Action Express (AE) cartridge is available, and there are at least three firms manufacturing .50 caliber handguns.[7] Any firearm larger than .50 caliber is classified by ATF as a destructive device that requires a special license for sale, manufacture, and possession. Hand grenades, bombs, and rockets are also included in the category of destructive devices. The relative stopping power (RSP) of the .50 AE cartridge is 385.[7] Compare this to an RSP of 5 for a .25 caliber, or of 58 for a 9 mm

TABLE 4.3 BODY ARMOR PROTECTION LEVELS[11]

Level of Protection	*Calibers Covered*
Type I Minimum level of protection, suitable for full-time wear.	.38 Special and .22 LRHV (long rifle, high velocity)
Type II-A Sufficiently comfortable for full- time wear	.357 Magnum JSP (jacketed soft point) and 9 mm FMJ (full metal jacket)
Type II Heavier and bulkier. May not be comfortable for full-time wear in hot and humid weather.	Higher velocity .357 JSP and 9 mm FMJ
Type III-A High velocity handgun and machine gun bullets. Highest level of protection as soft body armor, but not suitable for routine wear.	.44 Magnum lead SWC (semiwad cutter) gas-checked bullets and 9 mm FMJ
Type III High-powered rifle. Intended for use in tactical situations.	.308 Winchester FMJ bullets
Type IV Armor piercing rifle. Intended for use in tactical situations.	.30-06 AP (armor piercing bullets)

cartridge.[3] While relative stopping power is not necessarily the same as wounding potential, this ammunition is extremely powerful and, if it comes into common use, is likely to increase the probability of fatal injury from shootings.

GLASER SAFETY SLUG. This is a bullet with embedded lead shot so that on impact it inflicts tremendous tissue damage like that of a shotgun shell.[8] It is called a "safety slug" because it breaks apart on impact and does not ricochet. It also does not leave the body of the target, so injury to bystanders is in theory eliminated. These bullets are relatively expensive and so not widely used.[8] However, they can be purchased by anyone who follows state and local procedures for purchasing ammunition.

FLECHETTE. Some cartridges contain a dart-shaped projectile, called a flechette, instead of a bullet. Flechettes are typically longer, narrower, and lighter than the bullets they replace. This finned projectile has a high sectional density, or ratio of mass to surface area. Because it travels at a high velocity, a flechette's trajectory is generally flat and its depth of penetration is great. Cartridges with flechettes are expensive and not marketed widely to the civilian population.[13, 14]

CASELESS AMMUNITION. Some specialized rifles use an electric charge rather than a spark from a traditional primer to ignite the propellant.[13, 14] With such guns, the cartridge does not need to contain a primer. In addition, manufacturers have developed a propellant that is sticky rather than powdered so it adheres to itself and to the projectile. Together, the electric ignition and self-adhesive propellant make it possible to produce "caseless ammunition," cartridges that have no case and no primer. Although caseless ammunition was first introduced approximately fifty years ago, interest in this type of ammunition revives periodically. With traditional ammunition, law enforcement officers often use cartridge cases from a crime scene to determine the type of firearm that was used, and to link a recovered weapon to the crime by matching the markings on the recovered cases to markings on cases from test-fired cartridges. Use of caseless ammunition means that law enforcement officers will no longer be able to identify crime weapons by the cartridge cases left at the scene of the shooting, which is currently a very useful form of evidence.[13]

Emerging Technologies

LASER SIGHTS. Laser aiming devices, sometimes called laser sights, are available to attach to handguns and other firearms, or can be purchased as an integral part of the weapon. Laser sights increase the likelihood that an unskilled shooter can hit a target. More specifically, they increase an unskilled shooter's ability to "acquire" a target: that is, to place the gun's point of aim in the desired spot. Laser sights do not increase a gun's ability to accurately place a bullet, but they do help an unskilled shooter aim. Currently, laser sights cost under $200.

PLASTIC GUNS. In the late 1980s, plastic guns were widely discussed in the press. Some pundits feared that the development of a plastic that could withstand a cartridge's explosive forces meant that new guns might go undetected by metal detectors. Others were concerned that guns with plastic frames looked too much like toys and might be mistaken for toys by children. Following this discussion, a federal law passed that authorized the development of a "Security Exemplar" which would be shaped like a gun, have at least 3.7 ounces of stainless steel, and could be used to test and calibrate metal detectors. New guns manufactured after this law have to be at least as detectable as the Security Exemplar. Although all plastic guns were never a real technical possibility, some manufacturers do use high-tech polymers to reduce the size and weight of midcaliber and large-caliber weapons.[7] For example, Glock manufactures a 9 mm semiautomatic pistol whose frame is largely constructed of polymer, but whose barrel and other components are made of steel.

RECOIL-COMPENSATED HANDGUNS. Shooters have equipped their guns with "muzzle brakes" for at least a century, but the use of muzzle brakes on handguns appears to be gaining popularity.[7] Gas from the propellant typically exits straight out the muzzle, but a muzzle brake is a device that diverts some of the gas to the side or even to the rear, thereby reducing the recoil. A muzzle brake may be a device attached to the barrel of a firearm, or a pattern of holes cut into the barrel itself. On a handgun, the muzzle brake not only reduces the recoil, but it may also reduce muzzle jump, which is the firearm's tendency to move off of the point of aim at the moment of discharge. The effect is to make a large-caliber handgun considerably more manageable to shoot.[7]

Public Health Implication: Widespread use of more ammunition with greater wounding potential, of small but powerful handguns, and of laser sights which increase the shooter's accuracy pose a troubling possibility in the years ahead. These trends have the potential of increasing deaths and injuries, especially for assaults and homicides, fears of which appear to be fueling the increase in sales of guns for self-protection. At the same time, we do not have the institutional infrastructure to deal quickly or definitively with the distribution of these new technologies in the civilian population. Nor do we have the information that allows us to monitor the current or future impact of these technologies. The transfer of military technology, such as laser sights, to the civilian population could be halted but this is currently being done on an ad hoc basis by Congress at the federal level.[13] These topics are further discussed in Chapter 6.

Emerging Technologies

5

Injuries from Firearms

To understand how firearms produce injuries and how changes in firearm design can reduce injuries, it is helpful to know how the human body defends itself against injuries in general. The biomechanics of injury describe how the body responds to forces and how injuries result. The body's natural defenses—skin, bone, and muscle—are variously effective in dealing with different degrees of impact. For example, thick skin on the palms and soles protects the tissue underneath from the wear and tear of using our hands and feet. Other forces, such as from a fall, might cause a small bruise or a broken bone. The type and severity of the injury depends on the impact. Impact force is the sum of the forces created by the rate of impact (for example, the speed the body attains falling down stairs or off a bicycle), the place of impact (e.g., the knees, the hands, the back), the resistance of the place of impact (thick skin on the palms of the hands, for example), and the objects or surface hit on impact (e.g., concrete or grass).

In injury studies, impact forces are analogous to the virus, bacteria, or toxin that infectious disease studies address. And, just as scientists study the disease process to determine how to cure it, injury scientists look at the amount of impact force and how forces are dissipated within the body to seek ways of reducing injury. Falls were the first types of injury for which impact forces were measured. Soon, however, scientists were using the same concepts to measure the human tolerance for impact forces and forces generated in car crashes.[1, 2]

Once we understand the biomechanics of an injury, we can develop strategies to reduce the forces or change their effect on the body. Current studies of biomechanics in car crashes use crash-test dummies to measure forces that impact the head and other vulnerable body parts so that cars can be better designed. Important injury countermeasures came from such studies: seat belts and airbags to restrain the body during a crash, laceration-free windshields to keep the face from being badly cut, steering wheels and dashboards that cushion body parts rather than transferring energy to them.[3]

In earlier times, people believed that firearm injuries were caused by the lead bullet melting at impact or by injecting a poison into the body.[4] Scientists have since studied what happens to the body when a bullet hits it and how various bullets and firearms cause different kinds of injuries. These studies have been conducted by forensic pathologists who need to determine the identity of the bullet which killed their patient, by trauma physicians who need to know how best to repair injuries, and by military ballistics experts who are trying to improve the military capacity of weapons.

From the public health point of view, knowing how bullets cause injury allows us to plan and evaluate strategies to reduce damage in the civilian population. We are, however, a long way from easily translating into prevention strategies what we know about the biomechanics of firearm injuries. We present the information in this chapter as a starting point and to give readers a sense of the complexity of the issue.

Minimizing Damage versus Preventing Shootings

One way to reduce firearm injuries is to prevent the shooting. Another way is to reduce the likelihood or severity of an injury should a shooting occur. For car crashes, great strides in injury prevention were made when, in addition to working to reduce the number of crashes, people also began to work to reduce the number and severity of injuries that occurred during a crash by implementing seat belts and air bags, for example.

Guns and bullets were developed over time to increase damage. This may mean that strategies to prevent shootings in the first place will be most effective over the long term. Injury control concepts suggest, however, that exploring both strategies is important.

Where the Bullets Strike

Where the bullet strikes is the most important factor in firearm injury severity. A BB gun, an air rifle, or even a gun firing blanks can cause death by damaging the brain with the blast of expanding gas. The vulnerability of the human brain, the heart, and the great vessels makes the strategy of minimizing injuries in a shooting especially challenging.

Some parts of the body are extremely vulnerable to firearm or other penetrating injury. Injury to the brain and upper spinal cord—brain stem, basal ganglia, medulla oblongata, and the upper cervical spinal cord—is likely to cause immediate and total incapacitation. Injury to the frontal lobe of the brain can be lethal immediately if the bullet is large and high powered. Not all brain injuries are immediately lethal, though. A smaller caliber bullet can damage the frontal lobes and the victim still survive, though often with residual disabilities.

Injuries to other highly vulnerable parts of the body do not lead to instantaneous incapacitation, but may cause death within a minute or two. Depending on the caliber of the weapon, a firearm injury to the heart, aorta, or brain can be rapidly lethal. With a severe injury to the heart or aorta, the victim may retain a complete ability to function for ten to fifteen seconds, but the collapse of the circulatory system leads to death shortly after that.

Other organs and tissues such as the liver, kidney, and lungs bleed extensively with a firearm injury, but not as extensively as when the heart and aorta are injured. Rapid surgical intervention can stop the bleeding, and the injured person can survive.

Injuries to anatomic structures like bones and muscles are less likely to be life threatening. However, they can still require significant medical care and may produce disabilities. When gunshots wounds are not immediately lethal, the victim's survival depends on the rapid delivery of medical care at an appropriate facility, such as a trauma center, including blood and fluid replacement and surgical intervention. If the victim does not receive timely medical care, death will occur from blood loss and shock.

About 72 percent of people dying from gunshot wounds die before they reach the hospital.[5] For all gunshot fatalities, 40.5 percent result from wounds to the head, 30 percent result from wounds to the chest, 11 percent from wounds to the abdomen, and 18.5 percent from wounds to other sites.[5]

Public Health Implication: Very little of the research on gunshot injury biomechanics has been directed at answering public health questions. It is not clear to what extent the firearm injury problem might be affected by changing the design of weapons and ammunition or halting the trend toward more powerful ammunition and weapons. Important studies remain to be done to estimate the likelihood of death when shot with different kinds of weapons.

How Tissue Damage Occurs

Gunshot wounds damage tissue mostly through crushing and stretching. The severity and type of damage depends in part on the type of tissue affected.

A bullet crushes the tissue that is directly in its path. As a bullet penetrates the body it forms a path called the wound track. A perforating wound has both an entrance hole and an exit hole. A penetrating wound is one in which the bullet comes to rest in the body, making no exit hole.

A bullet can also damage tissue not directly in its path. As it decelerates, it transfers energy to the surrounding tissue, causing the tissue to stretch and deform. Muscle tissue is highly elastic and may return to its original shape after the stretching, leaving very little residual damage. Other tissue, such as brain and liver tissue, is not so elastic and may be permanently disrupted by the stretching.

As a bullet travels along the wound track, it shears, tears, or crushes the tissue it directly contacts, producing a permanent cavity that remains after the bullet has exited or come to rest.[6] The cavity fills with blood from the ruptured small and large blood vessels. Some bullets break into many fragments when they contact a target. Each fragment behaves like an individual missile, forming its own wound track.

Stretching forms a temporary cavity, which varies in size (depending on the caliber of the bullet) and reaches its maximum volume within fifty milliseconds of the bullet's passing through the tissue. The temporary cavity undulates for one-tenth to two-tenths of a second, depending on caliber, before collapsing. The cavity's width varies as a function of how much energy the bullet transfers to the tissue at each point along the way. Some tissue types are fairly resilient, but others, including bone and nonelastic organs like the liver and brain, may sustain serious damage during the formation of the temporary cavity.[6]

How Tissue Damage Occurs

The amount of tissue that is damaged depends on both the number of wounds and the characteristics of the bullet's shape and impact.

THE NUMBER OF WOUNDS. The more bullet wounds, the greater the likelihood a vital site has been hit. Multiple wounds make it harder for the physician to repair tissue in nonvital sites and increase the likelihood of complications. Therefore, the greater the number of wounds, the less likely the victim is to survive.

For a single wound, the amount of tissue damage will be determined by the degree of bullet penetration, the bullet's size, how big a path or wound track it makes, and whether it expands or fragments on impact. Each is discussed below.

Public Health Implication: Weapons with a larger magazine capacity and those that fire rapidly have a greater capability of inflicting multiple wounds. Large urban trauma centers report an increase in multiple gun shot wounds in trauma patients and a greater probability of the patient dying at the scene.[7] This has been attributed to an increase in use of high-caliber semiautomatic pistols.[8, 9]

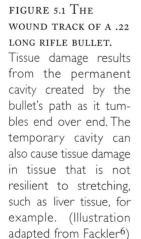

FIGURE 5.1 THE WOUND TRACK OF A .22 LONG RIFLE BULLET. Tissue damage results from the permanent cavity created by the bullet's path as it tumbles end over end. The temporary cavity can also cause tissue damage in tissue that is not resilient to stretching, such as liver tissue, for example. (Illustration adapted from Fackler[6])

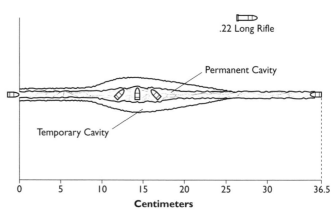

How Much Tissue Is Damaged

DEGREE OF BULLET PENETRATION. Bullets are designed and chosen for use, in part, with penetration and perforation in mind. If a bullet dissipates its energy quickly when it enters the body, it will not penetrate far.

Shotgun pellets are designed to be fired over a relatively short distances. Shotgun pellet penetration and perforation depends on shot size and the distance between the gun and the target. At close range, a shotgun blast produces extensive tissue damage over a relatively small area of the body and pellets may perforate the victim. At farther ranges, the shot disperses and loses velocity before hitting the target. The tissue damage is more diffuse, and the pellets do not penetrate as deeply.

A bullet that is high velocity and fully jacketed will sometimes pass cleanly through the body without dissipating its energy by deforming or tumbling end over end. Fully jacketed bullets are designed to penetrate deeply but they also perforate. If no vital organ is in the bullet's path there may be little tissue damage. However, these bullets can go on to wound another person.

Mushrooming or expanding bullets are designed to transfer a maximum amount of energy to the body and penetrate but not perforate. Depending on the site of impact, a vital organ such as in the liver or brain can be extensively damaged with relatively little penetration.

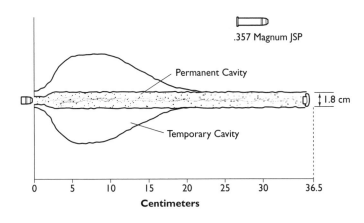

.357 Magnum JSP

Permanent Cavity

1.8 cm

Temporary Cavity

0   5   10   15   20   25   30   36.5
Centimeters

FIGURE 5.2 THE WOUND TRACK OF A .357 MAGNUM JACKETED SOFT-POINT BULLET. This bullet expands or mushrooms on impact with the body. It does not tumble, but its expanded size creates a large permanent cavity almost from the point of impact. (Illustration adapted from Fackler[6])

How Much Tissue Is Damaged

Law enforcement agents use expanding bullets because, if they must shoot someone, the bullet is less likely to perforate the intended target and go on to wound another person.

BULLET PATH SIZE. Path size is related to the kind of tissue in the bullet's path and to the bullet's profile at each point along the wound track. Tissues with different densities and elasticities respond to the bullet in different ways, as described earlier.

As a bullet creates a wound track, its profile is the amount of its surface area that comes into direct contact with tissue. If a high-velocity jacketed bullet hits an arm or lower leg and no bones are in its path, it creates a straight perforating wound through the body. In such a circumstance, the jacketed bullet has a relatively small profile at every point along the wound track that is no larger than the cross-sectional area of the bullet at its widest point. The resulting wound track is relatively narrow.[6]

However, a jacketed bullet may tumble within the body if its velocity is slow enough and its wound track is long enough, as is the case with most handgun wounds to the chest and abdomen. The bullet's center of gravity is behind the center of its long axis, making it inherently unstable. In flight, the bullet's rotational velocity stabilizes it, but this rotation stops when the bullet penetrates the body. Without the gyroscopic spin, nothing can keep the heaviest part, the base, from tumbling over the lightest part, the nose. The profile changes as the bullet penetrates the body, reaching its maximum at the point where the bullet's long axis is perpendicular to the wound track. (Figure 5.1)

An expanding bullet does not tumble because, once it has expanded, the heaviest part is at the front and the center of gravity is no longer behind the center of its long axis. Compared to jacketed bullets, expanding bullets cause more crushing and stretching at earlier points along the wound track. They decelerate rapidly along the part of the wound track that is closest to the entrance wound. (Figure 5.2)

There are several examples of expanding bullets of which the most extreme example is the Black Talon. The jacket of the original Black Talon expanded into a starburst shape with razor sharp edges. It was designed to have a very large profile as it traveled through the body. The bullet, when fully expanded, caused additional injury by cutting tissue with the sharp ends of its jacket. After trauma physicians raised concerns about the bullet, its manufacturer discontinued sales of the

How Much Tissue Is Damaged

original Black Talon to civilians. The bullet has since been modified to have duller edges and points and has been reintroduced for sale.[10] Several other manufacturers also produce bullets with expanding jackets for the civilian market.

Generally, bullets with a larger caliber will have a larger profile as they move through the body. These bullets also tend to have more power because they have greater mass. Thus, they tend to create wider permanent cavities. Higher velocity bullets also tend to create more extensive temporary cavities (See Figure 5.2).

Although jacketed and expanding bullets are designed to produce different effects, it is difficult to make general statements about which bullet design is more lethal. An expanding bullet maximizes cavitation and penetration: It creates relatively wider temporary and permanent cavities than does a jacketed bullet, but tends not to perforate the body as the jacketed bullet. Jacketed bullets threaten vital organs that are directly in the bullet's path. Cavitation from expanding bullets is a threat to vital organs that are closer to the entrance wound, even when the organs are not directly in the bullet's path.

The relative lethality of these two bullet designs is a question that cannot be answered without further study of the epidemiology of firearm injuries and deaths. These studies would be similar to those that helped identify the injury patterns of other products, cars and trucks, for example.

FIGURE 5.3 AN EXPANDED BLACK TALON BULLET. This bullet was designed to have a very large profile after impact. The razor sharp ends of the starburst-shaped jacket that expand on impact add additional cutting injury to the tissues it contacts. This bullet was voluntarily removed from the civilian market by its manufacturer after adverse publicity, but has since been reintroduced with duller edges and points.

Hollow-point bullets that expand on impact with the body are no longer used by the military, although they were developed especially by the military to increase casualties. Some people believe that infection rather than the bullet itself caused more casualties in military victims of hollow-point bullets. Up until World War II, infection had always posed a greater threat in the military setting than in the civilian setting. In the late 1800s, before aseptic surgery and antibiotics, a bullet that increased tissue damage

How Much Tissue Is Damaged

was particularly deadly in an environment in which infection was so significant a factor. For this reason, the Hague Convention of 1899 dictated that countries at war must not use bullets that cause undue pain and suffering, and the military use of expanding bullets came to an end.[4]

At higher velocities, some bullets fragment on impact with the target. The individual fragments do not penetrate as deeply as a single, unfragmented bullet, but the fragments disperse over a wider area in the body. Each fragment acts like an independent missile creating its own permanent and temporary cavity. Because the total surface area of the fragments is greater than that of an unfragmented bullet, more tissue is actually crushed and damaged.[4]

Energy Dissipation from a Bullet

A bullet's kinetic energy is determined by its mass and velocity when fired. Different weapons are designed to have different muzzle velocities (see Table 4.1). Handgun projectiles tend to have less velocity than rifle projectiles (typically 820 to 1,300 feet per second for handguns compared to 2,000 to 3,300 feet per second for rifles). The greater a bullet's velocity, the greater its kinetic energy, assuming the mass is held constant. This means that the higher velocity bullets tend to cause more tissue damage and often create larger and more disruptive temporary cavities. However, high-velocity jacketed bullets that create perforating wounds tend to cause little tissue damage as they dissipate little energy in the target and leave only a narrow permanent wound track. Among handgun cartridges, those with less velocity tend to produce less tissue damage when bullet designs are similar. Yet bullets of any caliber or velocity can be lethal by inflicting damage to vital organs.

BULLET CALIBER. Bullets of the same caliber may vary in shape, overall size, and weight. The bigger the bullet (e.g., the bigger the caliber) the more mass the bullet is likely to have. The more massive the bullet, the more kinetic energy it may acquire relative to other bullets. Because cartridges also vary in the amount and type of powder they contain, some large-caliber bullets acquire less velocity than some smaller-caliber bullets and, therefore, have less kinetic energy. As a general rule, however, if they strike the same body part, smaller-caliber handgun bullets produce less tissue damage than larger-caliber handgun bullets when the bullet design is similar.

Public Health Implications: Unfortunately, larger caliber handguns are playing an increasingly prominent role in the firearm injury problem. Many public health researchers and clinicians are calling attention to the growing frequency of wounds from larger caliber firearms and to the increasing proportion of firearm deaths resulting from larger caliber bullets.[8, 9, 11] This is a new and troubling dimension of the overall firearm injury problem and one that deserves attention. But, as we search for strategies to stem this burgeoning problem, we must be careful to avoid the assumption that small-caliber bullets are risk free. Small-caliber bullets (.22 and .25) are associated with a substantial proportion of homicides and suicides—26 percent of all firearms deaths in Milwaukee from 1990 through 1994.[11] It may take one set of strategies to reduce the rates of injury and death from small-caliber handguns and another to reduce the rates of injury and death from large-caliber handguns, but clearly both need to be pursued. For public health professionals the challenge has always been to find an effective combination of strategies to counter a multifaceted problem.

Nonlethal Ammunition

Not all ammunition is lethal. To be lethal or cause injury, ammunition has be fired with enough energy to penetrate the skin and has to be made of a material that exceeds the injury thresholds of human skin, bone, and muscle. Law enforcement agencies and military units use nonlethal ammunition that, although it is fired from a gun, is not designed to penetrate beyond soft tissue. One example is rubber bullets, which are both too big and too soft to penetrate human skin easily.[4] Another type of nonlethal ammunition is a cartridge of tear gas or pepper gas fired from handguns. Guns which fire gas cartridges are commonly used for self-protection in Europe, but are illegal in the United States.

Public Health Implication: One strategy that might reduce deaths and injuries from firearms would be to encourage, by many means, the substitution of nonlethal for lethal ammunition. This might be part of a broader strategy suggested by public health researchers of encouraging the use of less lethal means of self-protection than firearms.[12]

The study of what happens when bullets enter the body is called wound ballistics. Understanding wound ballistics of different kinds of ammunition and different weapons can help public health personnel predict which of those are more likely to be involved in injuries or deaths. This technical information helps people determine which weapons and ammunitions might need special policies addressing their modification, restriction, or banning.

Specialists in wound ballistics use several models for the human body when they try to determine a bullet's effects: soap, gelatin, wood, or animal cadavers. Additional research and development of appropriate models, including computer models, would help immensely in determining the biomechanics of impact injuries.

Most wound ballistics research has been conducted in military laboratories, which are interested in maximizing wounding. Just as we developed crash-injury research laboratories and crash-test dummies to determine how to protect people in car crashes, we need to support and develop wound ballistics studies aimed at reducing or preventing injury.

Although we have some information on the effect of bullets striking targets in laboratory settings, there is little real-world epidemiologic information linking the firearms, bullets, and wounds. Such information would help us translate the laboratory findings into injury prevention countermeasures, which can lead to changes in public health policies.

6

Where Guns Come From

In this chapter, we change our focus from guns as individual objects and the damage they do, to guns as products that are manufactured, marketed, sold, purchased, stolen, and used. When we look at changing a product associated with public health problems, we need to understand enough about the industry and its directions to see which strategies might be most effective. From a public health perspective, the tensions of regulating the production and use of potentially hazardous goods like firearms in a market-driven economy are similar to those of regulating pesticides, tobacco, and alcohol. But, tobacco, pesticide, and alcohol use and control have been studied and researched extensively, unlike firearm use.

We present an overview in this chapter of firearm manufacture, distribution, and ownership. As we have done in other chapters, we include information on the public health implications of our material. Regulations and federal laws are mentioned from time to time throughout this chapter, but are discussed more fully in Chapter 7.

How Many Guns Are There?

No one knows for sure how many guns there are in the United States. A commonly cited estimate places the number at about two hundred and thirty million, but this figure is the total number of all guns imported and produced in the United States since 1900. Since not all of these guns are likely to remain in working order nor even still to exist, the number is surely smaller.[1] Still, four to five million new guns are manufactured in the U.S. each year.[2] Law enforcement agencies frequently destroy firearms they confiscate, but that amounts to only a hundred thousand per year or so.[1]

Public Health Implication: Guns are common. Clearly, some guns in some situations are more likely to cause death and injury than others. Epidemiologists look for patterns—how products are used, when they're used, how they perform, who uses them, what problems are related to their use, whether particular aspects of a product stand out, among other things. We need to increase the amount of scientific research to identify these patterns for firearms to have a guide for developing social policy and health education so we can reduce deaths and injuries.

Manufacture of Guns

Firearms are manufactured products. Information on the trends and characteristics of firearm manufacturing can help us to understand the origins of the firearms that are now widely available in the United States. While we do not intend for this to be a definitive description of the firearm industry, we highlight some important trends that have special relevance for injury control.

The production and importation of firearms since World War II is reflected in the Figures 6.1, 6.2, and 6.3 which show the combined effects of manufacturers' marketing decisions, public and military

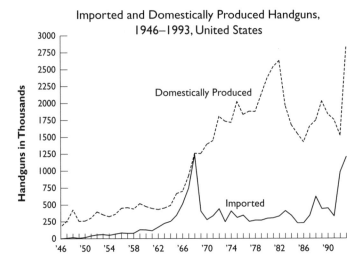

FIGURE 6.1

Manufacture of Guns

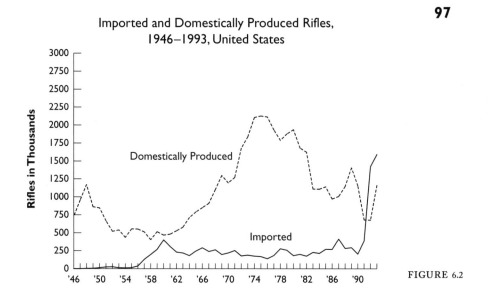

Imported and Domestically Produced Rifles, 1946–1993, United States

FIGURE 6.2

FIGURES 6.1, 6.2, 6.3 THE DOMESTIC PRODUCTION AND IMPORT OF HANDGUNS, RIFLES, AND SHOTGUNS IN THE YEARS FROM THE END OF WORLD WAR II TO 1993. Increases in 1993 are thought to be due to manufacturers stockpiling firearms prior to anticipated changes in federal regulations. (Information is from the Bureau of Alcohol, Tobacco, and Firearms.)

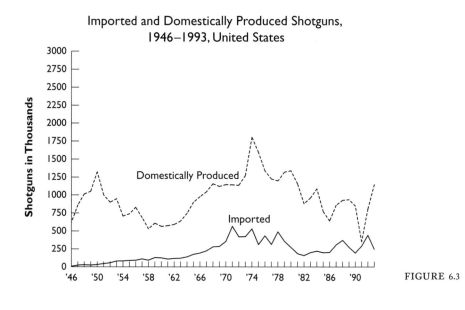

Imported and Domestically Produced Shotguns, 1946–1993, United States

FIGURE 6.3

Manufacture of Guns

demand, and federal and state regulations regarding gun production or gun use. While we present information on rifles and shotguns as well as handguns, we spend more time discussing handguns because of their important role in firearm injuries and deaths.

Gun Control Act of 1968

The provisions of the federal Gun Control Act of 1968 set strict criteria on importing handguns, but not for those produced domestically. (See Appendix 1 for a description of these import criteria.) Effects of the act can be seen both in the sharp peak of imports in 1967 in anticipation of its provisions and in the rise of production of handguns in the United States.[3] From 1946 to 1968, handguns accounted for 24 percent of firearms produced in the U.S. The proportion increased to 38 percent from 1969 through 1981, and to 50 percent from 1982 though 1993.[2]

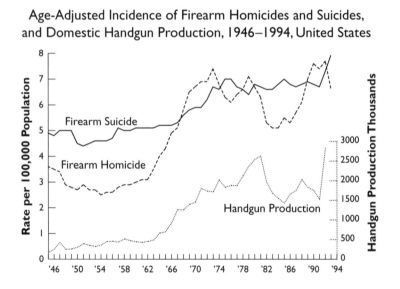

Age-Adjusted Incidence of Firearm Homicides and Suicides, and Domestic Handgun Production, 1946–1994, United States

FIGURE 6.4 The domestic handgun production rate parallels the homicide rate in the United States. The death rates have been adjusted for changes in the population. (Mortality data from 1994 are provisional estimates from the National Center for Health Statistics; handgun production data from the ATF.)

Gun Control Act

Public Health Implication: Firearm homicide rates parallel domestic handgun production.[3] Firearm suicides, on the other hand, show a steadier increase. (Figure 6.4) Evidence that compares manufacturing trends with diseases and injury has been often used to associate cause of death with consumer products, such as rising sales of tobacco products with increases in lung cancer and heart disease, or international comparisons of sales of food products that imply changes to a Western diet with an increase in heart disease in countries where heart disease has traditionally been rare. While such associations do not imply cause and effect, they have been important epidemiologic clues.

Industry Responses to Decreased Sales in Early 1980s

Firearm sales decreased in the early 1980s, as reflected in the decreased production of all firearms. The Bureau of Alcohol, Tobacco, and Firearms (ATF), the source of these data, tracks production and import figures, but no actual sales data are available.

The industry's analysis of the sales slump was that their traditional market was saturated. The white, older, males who had been mainstay customers were no longer buying new weapons.[1, 4] The designs of revolvers, shotguns, and rifles had remained essentially unchanged since the late nineteenth century, so once the market was saturated, there was nothing new to entice gun owners to replace their existing supply.[1] The firearm industry responded by creating new marketing strategies to sell guns to women and to promote the sale of guns for self-protection rather than game hunting.[4] Advertisements reflecting these strategies are described later in this chapter.

Industry also responded by introducing and heavily marketing new technologies. For example, the Glock 17, an expensive semiautomatic pistol with a polymer frame, was introduced in 1986 and quickly stirred interest and sales with its new look.[1] In addition to its lightweight yet durable construction, its seventeen-round magazine contrasted dramatically with a more typical seven-round capacity.[1] To spur sales, firearm manufacturers also made as much as possible of the endorsements implied by military contracts or media exposure. Selection of the semiautomatic 9 mm Beretta pistol in 1985 as the sidearm for the military was accompanied by higher sales of this model in the civilian population.[1]

Industry Responses to Decreased Sales

Sales were also reportedly fueled by a spate of mid-1980s television shows in which large caliber semiautomatic weapons figured heavily in the plots, *Miami Vice,* for example.[5]

Advertising

Gun manufacturer advertising is part of what drives consumer demand in all markets. Compilations show advertisements using "fear based" marketing.[6] Guns are being sold for self-protection with lines like: "Home-owner's Insurance"; "Handguns you can bet your life on"; "Self-protection is not only your right, it's your responsibility." This line is depicted with a woman bending over a child in bed as if to say good night. It likens gun ownership to keeping a fire extinguisher in the house. The "self-protection" ad was printed in the *Ladies Home Journal,* but only those distributed in selected regions of the country.[6] It has been at the center of many discussions of marketing campaigns newly aimed at women.[4]

Many ads emphasize the small size of the weapon and its easy concealability. Or they show weapons in night stand drawers, in purses, or on top of bedroom furniture, implying that having a gun in easy reach will protect the family. Such pictures also imply that the gun should be kept loaded and accessible.

Promoting guns for self-protection seems to have increased since the mid-1980s when handgun manufacturers were in a sales slump.[1, 4] This is coupled with a niche marketing campaign aimed at women as firearms manufacturers tried to overcome the market saturation of guns among white males.[4] Ads aimed at women stress the women's need for protection from strangers intent upon harm, whereas the data suggest that women are twice as likely to be killed by male intimates using guns as by strangers using any means.[4]

Public Health Implication: The scientific evidence is that keeping a gun in the home, and keeping it loaded, increases the risk of unintentional shooting by children, of suicide, and of homicide to family members.[7, 8, 9] Public health and medical groups have asked the Federal Trade Commission to act on gun advertising that depicts guns in hazardous situations, such as night stands, or makes claims about the use of guns for self-protection.[10] Activists contend that this amounts to misleading advertising. The risks of keeping guns in the home are discussed more at the end of this chapter.

Guns are a product and are marketed to create consumer demand. As a society we have chosen to monitor and restrict tobacco and alcohol advertising to try to reduce their use by vulnerable populations like children. We also require that other consumer products do not make false or misleading claims in their advertisements. This social choice could be extended to firearms.

The New Saturday Night Special

The large-caliber, semiautomatic pistols are generally expensive. A segment of the industry based in California has developed and marketed small, inexpensive, and small-caliber semiautomatic pistols.[11, 12] These guns are inexpensive to produce. They are often made from a zinc alloys that are softer than the steel alloys used for higher quality weapons. In tests conducted by gun magazines, they are often described as "junk" because they routinely jam or misfire.[11]

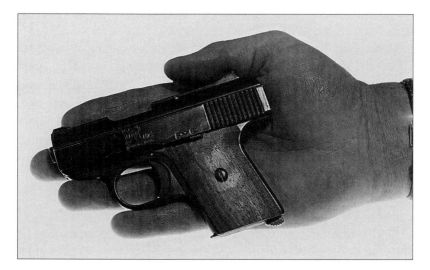

FIGURE 6.5 The RAVEN MP 25. This is a .25 caliber, seven-shot semiautomatic pistol made by Phoenix Arms. It is easily concealed and is inexpensive to manufacture, under $20. Consider it to be a modern Saturday Night Special. In one city, it was the single most commonly identified gun used in homicides and suicides.[13]

New Saturday Night Special

FIGURE 6.6 THE LORCIN 38. Manufactured by one of the family companies (Lorcin Engineering) that also produces the Raven, the Lorcin chambers .38 caliber cartridges and is considered a midsize caliber. It is approximately the same size as the Raven pictured in Figure 6.5, and is also inexpensively priced. It is also a Saturday Night Special.

The California companies—Davis Industries, Lorcin Engineering, Phoenix Arms, Bryco Arms, and Sundance Industries—the fastest growing segment of the industry, currently lead in .25 caliber semi-automatic pistol production.[11] They are shifting production over to higher powered, but still small and easily concealed, .380 and 9 mm semiautomatic pistols such as the Raven and the Lorcin 38 pictured here.[11] Hoping to repeat the success of these companies, major old-line manufacturers are beginning to produce similar guns.[14]

Public Health Implication: Guns manufactured by the "Ring of Fire" California companies are heavily marketed by their manufac-turers as being useful for self-protection and easy to conceal, despite their unreliability.[11] Their current strategy appears to be to increase production of small, and ever-more-powerful handguns without substantially increasing the price. This trend may be asso-ciated with an increase in deaths and injuries from firearms.[11]

New Saturday Night Special

The Rise of the Semiautomatic Pistol

Marketing, new technologies, and new companies have resulted in a dramatic change in handgun manufacture since the early 1980s. Revolvers, long the most common kind of handgun, are now out-produced by semiautomatic pistols.[14, 15] In domestic production, the revolver has decreased from a 65 percent market share in 1980 to 22 percent in 1994.[2] (Figure 6.7) Almost all the growth in pistol production has been in medium- and large-caliber guns—for example, domestic manufacture of 9 mm semiautomatic weapons has increased more than tenfold over the last ten years.[2] (Figure 6.8)

Recent Changes in Manufacturing Trends

The industry responded to the possibility of increased federal regulation of firearms after the 1992 elections and change in presidential administration. Domestic manufacture of all firearms increased sharply in 1993. ATF attributes this to manufacturers rushing production

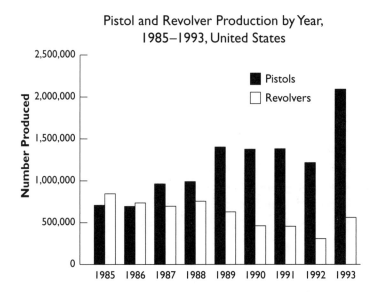

FIGURE 6.7 Semiautomatic pistols have replaced revolvers as the handgun most commonly produced in the United States during the past decade. The revolver has decreased from a 65 percent market share in 1980 to 22 percent in 1994.

Rise of the Semiautomatic Pistol

U.S. Production of 9 mm Pistols, 1985–1994

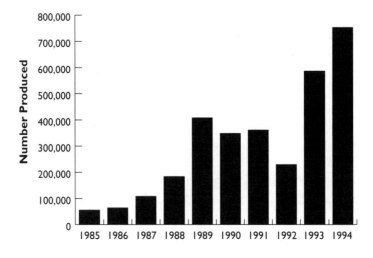

FIGURE 6.8 Most of the growth in semiautomatic pistol production has been in midsize and large-caliber guns. The domestic manufacture of 9 mm weapons has increased tenfold in the past decade. The diagram includes pistols more than .380 caliber up to 9 mm Parabellum. (From ATF Annual Firearms Manufacturing Report.)

before anticipated federal legislation so their existing stock could be "grandfathered" as legal, if necessary.

Import of rifles increase as well in 1992 and 1993, reflecting the approval of China and Russia as sources of arms. Weapons import from China was proscribed in 1994, and that from Russia was curtailed. Trade policy discussions in mid-1996 resulted in Russia once again being allowed to export rifles and handguns to the United States, with a predicted large increase in imports of Russian firearms.[16]

Future Trends

Several technologies, described in Chapter 3, are converging to produce powerful semiautomatic pistols that are easier to use than previous models.[14] There are the double-action-only pistols. They are designed to be operated without external safety devices are promoted as "draw and shoot" weapons. There are weapons with recessed hammers, which are

Future Trends

less likely to snag on clothing or holsters. They are marketed as quick-
draws. Finally, there are recoil compensators, which reduce the "kickback" of very large caliber pistols, thus increasing their ease of use and their appeal to some purchasers.[14] The promotion of quick-draw firearms appears to be an industry response to the changes in state laws that make it easier to obtain a license for carrying concealed weapons.[14]

Public Health Implication: The promotion of firearms that are easy to use, easy to conceal, and more powerful may increase the sales of these weapons. We are concerned that more injuries will follow. More severe injuries were reported after high-caliber, semiautomatic weapons were introduced in some communities.[17, 18, 19]

Gun manufacturers face no restrictions in incorporating technological advances into their products nor in promoting them to all markets. As a nation, we have not established the means by which to readily measure the effect of these advances, nor do we have an expedient means to restrict their promotion or use.

Distribution of Guns

Once weapons are manufactured, various distribution systems, both legal and illegal, work to bring them into people's hands. The Bureau of Alcohol, Tobacco, and Firearms (ATF) has regulatory authority from the federal government to oversee the system, to monitor legal sales, and to try to disrupt illegal sales and markets.

Public Health Implication: The main role of ATF is to oversee the distribution system for firearms rather than to set standards for their manufacture, quality, safety, and public health risk. It does have enforcement authority over the few standards for gun manufacture that have been set forth in federal law, such as the minimum barrel lengths for rifles and shotguns, and conversion of semiautomatic firearms to fully automatic. Expansion of its authority to include setting standards for manufacture has been proposed by many public health professionals.[1, 15]

The Gun Control Act of 1968 established a federal firearm licensing system which is administered by the Bureau of Alcohol, Tobacco, and Firearms in the Department of the Treasury. Firearm and ammunition manufacturers and importers must apply for federal firearm licenses (FFLs) before they can set up a business. Firearm dealers must do the same. A dealer's license permits an individual or business to sell guns and to purchase them from wholesalers or by mail. Until recently, the requirements for obtaining an FFL were simple: $10 per year for a three-year license and certification that the applicant was not a felon, mentally unstable, nor an illegal alien. The ease with which this license could be obtained and the privileges it carried meant that the number of federally licensed firearm dealers grew from about 150,000 in 1975 to close to 250,000 in 1993.[20]

In 1993 and 1994 the requirements for obtaining a dealer's license became more stringent. Applicants must now submit a photograph and a set of fingerprints with the application form. They must also certify that the business will be conducted in compliance with state and local laws, and notify local law enforcement of their intent to obtain a Federal Firearms License. Indications are that making the requirements more stringent and increasing fees from $30 to $200 for three years has significantly decreased the number of applications and renewals. The number of licensees shrank from almost 250,000 at the end of 1993 to 150,000 at the end of 1995.[21] That is still 600 dealers for each of the 250 ATF inspectors available to oversee their compliance with federal regulations.

Licensed firearms dealers are not all commercial businesses. An ATF study in 1993 showed that about 25 percent of them conducted business in a commercial site, but only 6 percent of the total had a volume of business that suggested a true retail establishment—buying or selling more than fifty guns a year.[22] Many of these individuals sell guns out of their homes—so called "kitchen table" dealers—or at gun shows and flea markets. The 150,000 FFLs should be contrasted with the 16,000 gun store owners who are part of an industry trade association, the National Association of Stocking Gun Dealers. This group is interested in putting these kitchen table dealers out of business. They see them as competitors and describe them as a "government-created black market."[23]

Public Health Implication: By establishing a federal firearm licensing system, we have made a social decision that selling firearms is not a casual business. An analogy to the ATF overseeing FFLs might be a city health department overseeing restaurants in order to control the spread of infectious diseases. However, the social decision to regulate sales practices for weapons does not extend to substantive product regulation. This is akin to our social decision to regulate the sale, but not the production of tobacco.

The Federal Firearms Licensee is expected to follow federal, state, and local ordinances in weapon sales. This includes ensuring that sales comply with state laws where the purchaser lives as well as those where the sale is made. Each purchaser of a weapon is required to complete a form (Form 4473, see Appendix 2) with their name and address, and information on the make, model, and serial number of the weapon. The form asks the purchaser to certify (by signing) that he or she is not a felon, has never been adjudged mentally incompetent nor committed to a mental institution, is not addicted to drugs, and is not an illegal alien. Since 1994, it is unlawful for a person to give or sell a handgun or ammunition to a juvenile under age eighteen or for a juvenile to possess a handgun or ammunition. Recent provisions of federal law also make it illegal to transfer or sell a firearm to anyone under a court order for domestic abuse. The dealer is required to keep Form 4473 on the premises and must allow the ATF to view it in routine inspections or when tracing a weapon for a criminal investigation.

Public Health Implication: By law, Form 4473 is neither collected centrally, nor are data from it stored on computer. The reasons are to avoid the appearance of "firearm registration" and to limit the ability of government to know who owns a firearm. This policy, fostered by the National Rifle Association, is based on a fear that, if government knew where all the weapons were, it could more easily confiscate them. Decentralization limits law enforcement access to valuable information on firearms sales and ownership. It also prevents public health researchers from using the data to evaluate risk factors associated with weapons and injuries. By comparison, registration of motor vehicles is routine in all states for all citizens and it does not interference in their civil liberties. Information from car registration data has been invaluable in assessing the relationships between motor vehicle designs and injuries in crashes.

Illegal Sales and Theft

The Bureau of Alcohol, Tobacco, and Firearms is responsible for enforcing laws regarding firearms sale and transfer. Despite relatively easy legal access to guns in this country, there is active illegal gun trafficking.[23, 24] Some dealers have used the FFL to get guns through the mail and sell them without following even the minimal procedures required to assure that purchasers were not felons, or without examining the state laws where the purchasers lives. Some legally buy quantities of weapons, take them to areas with more restrictive laws, and sell them on the street.[24, 25]

We have little information on the numbers and kinds of infractions of legal sales. But in the existing system, purchasing a weapon is quite easy. Furthermore, as the ATF has limited personnel, it is difficult for them to enforce what laws do exist that cover the sales of guns, so it is easy even to sell guns illegally.

According to criminologists, predatory criminals often do not obtain their guns from legitimate dealers. They get them from acquaintances, family members, and street sources.[24, 25] Yet legitimate sources are also important. In a survey of state prison inmates, nearly one quarter had gotten their guns from a retail source.[26] Regardless, every gun sold on the black market was, at one time, legally manufactured and sold to a dealer.

Public Health Implication: We do not know the relative proportions of weapons obtained legally or illegally that are associated with homicides, suicides, and unintentional deaths and injuries. Are guns that are illegally obtained more likely to be used in crimes? Does disrupting the illegal market affect homicides more than carefully regulating the existing legal markets? What would be the effect on deaths and injuries of reducing the overall number of guns available to the black market? Answers to these questions would help law enforcement agencies direct their resources.

Theft also brings guns into the black market. Not only do thefts from dealers occur, but thefts also occur during robberies from people who may have purchased a weapon legally. One estimate from the National Crime Victimization Survey is that annually 350,000 thefts involve at least one gun, or about 190,000 handguns and 160,000 long guns. This does not include thefts from dealers or instances where more than one gun was stolen.[27] The number of handguns stolen a year (190,000) is about 10 percent of the annual domestic production of handguns.

Public Health Implication: Some manufacturers are developing "personalized" guns that cannot be fired except by an authorized user. These guns are being advertised both for their safety, preventing unintentional injury to children, and for their theft deterring factor, because the gun would be useless to anyone but the owner.

Where firearms are readily accessible, firearm prices in illegal markets tend to be lower than in the legal market. On the other hand, in jurisdictions that control weapons more tightly, limiting legal access, gun-running from other jurisdictions produces substantial profit. For example, in the early 1990s a .25 caliber handgun could be bought for $35 or less on a Milwaukee street corner, for $60 in a Milwaukee gun shop, and for $300 on a New York City street corner. Similar price disparities are observed in other parts of the country.[24] In New York City a person cannot purchase a handgun without obtaining a permit to do so.

Public Health Implication: The public health community has advocated using taxation to increase price as a tool for reducing both tobacco and alcohol use. It is likely that taxing weapons would decrease their availability and their attraction in some segments of the population. However, we need more information to know how to target taxes effectively, both for high-risk populations and high-risk weapons.

The Gray Market and the Secondary Market

There is also an active gray market—sales and swaps at gun shows, by word of mouth, and through classified ads. Currently, a person holding an FFL can establish a business anywhere he chooses as long as no state or local ordinances prohibit the sale. Ample evidence shows that most FFL dealers do not operate retail gun shops, but sell in these informal situations.[22] Many dealers in this market do not comply with state and local regulations; however, the market is difficult to monitor for infractions.

Guns routinely change hands in this country through sales or informal loans and swaps among friends and relatives. This "secondary market" is part of what supplies guns for youth, because federal law prohibits those under eighteen from possessing a handgun. Several surveys indicate that many high school students either bring a gun to school, have a gun at home, or know where they could obtain a gun.[28, 29]

> **Public Health Implication:** Who owns the guns that injure people? How does this vary for suicide, homicide, and unintentional injury? By age of the victim? By age of the shooter? In one study of motor vehicle crashes, fewer than 25 percent of people injured were the original purchasers.[30] Individuals make decisions whether to own a gun, and if so, what its characteristics and optional safety equipment will be. These decisions ultimately affect many others. These are researchable questions and ones whose answers might guide policy.

Gun Ownership and Usage

Unlike automobiles, whose ownership is recorded by state agencies and tracked by insurance companies, firearms are not kept track of in any centralized manner. What little we know about who owns guns and why comes from surveys. The Gallup Poll and the National Opinion Research Center, for example, often do polls on gun ownership. Information also comes from other, similar regional polls. These rarely collect information on the type, model, or caliber of weapon, but occasionally they differentiate between long gun ownership and handgun ownership.

At the end of 1993, about 49 percent of households in the United States reported to Gallup that they possessed a gun.[24] Although this percentage has not changed since 1959 when such polls began, the number of households with *handguns* has increased substantially, from 13 percent in 1959 to about 32 percent.[24]

The number of gun owners varies by region. More guns are owned in southern/south-central states and in western/mountain states.[23] Historically, gun ownership has been more common in rural areas and in sparsely populated western states. Such geographic variation in gun ownership coincides with rates of use of guns in homicides, suicides, and violent crimes.[31]

Reasons for gun ownership are changing. Guns were owned by white men, and they were owned primarily for hunting and other sporting purposes. In recent years, the proportion of the population that hunts has decreased. Furthermore, the hunting population is aging and apparently is not being replaced completely by younger hunters. Simultaneously, gun ownership in urban areas is increasing, and urban gun owners report that they own guns for self-protection.

Public Health Implication: With the hunting population in decline and gun ownership for self-protection increasing, there will be proportionally fewer long guns than handguns. This increase of handguns creates an increased risk for deaths and injuries because there are more guns whose intended target is the human being.

In Wisconsin, a state with an active hunting population, half the households report having guns. But 56 percent reported having only long guns and 5 percent reported owning only handguns.[32] Of Wisconsin gun owners, 44 percent reported keeping all guns locked and unloaded. Others reported that some, but not all, guns were locked and unloaded, or guns were locked and loaded. Forty percent reported guns stored unlocked and unloaded.[32] A national survey of randomly selected gun owners found that among handgun owners, those who kept guns for self-protection and those who had no children at home were more likely to keep guns stored loaded and unlocked.[33]

Public Health Implication: Storage practices of firearms are often the focus of gun safety education programs. There are little data to show the overall effect of safety programs on gun storage. Nor are there data on the relative risks of different kinds of injuries related to gun storage practices. Information on both is essential to creating effective public health education programs on firearms.

Gun Ownership and Usage

Although guns are marketed and bought for self-protection, the available data suggest that guns confer risk not protection. For every justifiable homicide in which a handgun was used, there are ninety-five other homicide and suicide deaths involving handguns.[1] From a survey we know that even when a gun is in the home, only 3 percent of victims bring a gun to bear in their defense against an intruder or someone attempting to break in.[27] Although guns are found in about 50 percent of U.S. households, having a gun in the house doesn't necessarily mean that a crime victim will be able to use it successfully in self-defense.[4]

The myth that guns provide protection may be particularly deadly. Evidence is mounting that keeping a gun in the home increases the risk of death by homicide, suicide, or accident to those who live there. Risks of suicide are increased almost by five and risks of homicide almost triple.[7, 8]

Public Health Implication: To understand the relationships, if any, among high-risk situations, firearms, and populations, we must compare events and populations where injuries occur to those where they do not. Arthur Kellermann and co-authors used this traditional epidemiologic design to look at guns in the home. The study identified gun ownership, especially handgun ownership, as a separate and strong indicator of higher homicide risk, finding that homicides are almost three times as likely to occur when there is a gun in the home. The homicides were almost entirely committed by family members or intimate acquaintances, not strangers.[7] For homicides, they also found that households which included an illicit drug user, a person with prior arrests, or a person who had previously been hit or struck during a fight in the home were at higher risk. When Kellermann and his co-authors studied suicide, they found that risk factors included living alone, taking psychotropic medication, arrest records, and alcohol and drug abuse. The presence of a gun in the home, though, controlling for differences in the other risk factors, increased the risk of suicide by almost five.[8] Another study using similar methods found the risk of completed suicide by troubled adolescents doubled when guns were available in the home, even if the guns were locked.[34] More studies of these types will be necessary to establish the risks of gun ownership in specific situations, with specific outcomes, and with specific weapons.

One criminologist has been asserting that guns are used 2.5 million times per year to ward off crime.[35] Other criminologists question this assertion, supporting their counterclaims with evidence from the National Crime Victimization Survey, the FBI's Uniform Crime Reports, and data from death certificates. A survey in April 1994 shows that only 1 percent of all victims of violence, including law enforcement agents—altogether an estimated 62,000 people—claim to have used any firearm at all in self-defense.[27] An additional 20,000 reported using a firearm to defend against theft. There is a significant disparity of numbers between these 82,000 people and the 2.5 million claimed by this criminologist.[4] Compare, as well, the magnitude of 82,000 people who use firearms to defend themselves to the 931,000 victims of violent crimes committed with guns reported in the same survey.

Many people own guns. The risks of death and injury to self and family increases if guns are kept in homes. As with other products that are potentially hazardous, we need to understand the benefits and risks of gun ownership so that individuals can make choices based on adequate information.

Public Health Implication: In public health, education is used to inform people about risks they face when they choose to smoke, drink alcoholic beverages, eat fatty meats, and own guns. The better we are at describing high-risk situations, high-risk weapons, and high-risk populations for deaths and injuries from firearms, the more specific our public health strategies can be. Alternatively, for people seeking self-protection through guns, a public health response might be to describe the risks and benefits of guns for self-protection and to encourage other, less lethal, means to do the same job. Public health education based on sound scientific information and marketed appropriately has changed eating, smoking, exercise, and drinking habits among some segments of the population. In doing so, it has also changed social behavior and provided impetus for public policy change. These actions did not come without substantial effort and prolonged debate in the academic literature and popular media.

Guns for Self-Protection

Recognizing that firearm deaths and injuries are problems that can be addressed from the public health perspective is a substantial and positive step. Changing the way we address a problem should result in fresh and innovative research and programs, and, eventually, in new and better policy. The information in this chapter is analogous to an infectious disease expert's description of the human behaviors and social practices which affect disease transmission. We have some clues about what might prevent increase and spread of guns and the concurrent increased risk of injuries and death from guns, and we should have some ideas about directions for future research, demonstration projects, or public policies.

7

How Guns Are Currently Regulated

What are the laws that currently govern the manufacture, sale, and possession of firearms? In this chapter, we provide a brief overview, concentrating on federal laws and regulations that apply to firearm manufacture. Because the Second Amendment is often cited in support of unrestricted access to firearms, we discuss it briefly.

The information here provides at best the highlights of an extraordinarily complex area and may seem superficial to people well versed in legal matters. Readers desiring more information on legal principles behind the laws and product liability suits will find a thorough discussion in *Protecting the Public: Legal Issues in Injury Prevention* by Thomas Christoffel and Stephen Teret.[1]

For other readers, this brief introduction to the current regulatory landscape supplies a context for the strategies for changes discussed in Chapter 8.

The Second Amendment

Although it may be debated elsewhere, there is widespread agreement among public health legal experts that the Second Amendment to the United States Constitution does not give each United States citizen the right to own a gun.[2] The Second Amendment reads:

> *A well regulated Militia, being necessary to the security of a free State, the right of the people to keep and bear Arms, shall not be infringed.*

Court cases make clear that the Second Amendment applies to state-organized militias, not individual citizens or informal groups that call themselves militias.[2] No federal court has found any existing gun law to be in violation of the amendment. Nor does this amendment prohibit state gun laws. In fact, the federal government and all fifty states have laws that regulate the use, possession, sale, and manufacture of firearms. For further information, the legal principles and court rulings about the Second Amendment are described in a thoroughly reasoned and carefully written article titled *Firearms and Health: The Right to be Armed with Accurate Information about the Second Amendment*, by public health legal experts Jon Vernick and Stephen Teret.[2]

An Overview of Current Laws and Regulations

Three levels of government regulate guns: federal, state, and local. Federal law supersedes any contradictory state or local laws.[1] Thus, federal laws affecting guns must be followed throughout the nation. After those laws, state and local laws can vary widely, however.

Brief Overview of Federal Law

Federal legislation affecting guns has been enacted in response to social issues in the country's recent history. In the 1930s, gangster violence led to laws restricting general civilian use of several kinds of weapons. In the late 1960s, urban riots and political assassinations led to changes in gun importation law and created the system for federally licensing and regulating sales, which is still in place today. And, most recently, urban violence and frequent mass murders in public settings like restaurants, commuter trains, schools, and workplaces led to more recent legislation restricting manufacture and sales of high-capacity firearms. Much of this legislation has attempted to restrict access to types of guns and ammunition thought to be particularly hazardous. Often it has addressed specifically those problems receiving the most press attention. Instead of taking a comprehensive approach to problems of firearm deaths and injuries, federal firearm regulation has been ad hoc, responding to more immediate concerns.[3] Unlike most consumer products—motor vehicles, household appliances, toys, medicines—no single federal agency has administrative responsibility for firearms to keep excise taxes current with inflation, to set minimum safety standards for domestically manufactured guns and ammunition, or to determine if new technologies in firearms, ammunition, and accessories may injure civilian public health and safety.

The Bureau of Alcohol, Tobacco, and Firearms in the Treasury Department has jurisdiction over some aspects of firearm sale and manufacture, but its authority does not include regulating firearms as consumer products.[3] Legislation establishing the Consumer Product Safety Commission (CPSC) in 1972 does provide authority for government-established safety standards, recalls of defective products, and prohibition of sales of unsafe products, but the CPSC is specifically excluded from exercising jurisdiction over firearms.[3]

The highlights of federal laws pertaining to firearms are described here to show that firearm manufacture, sale, and possession have all been previously regulated in some fashion. We note some instances when the law's language meant that it could be circumvented, lessening its impact. Readers seeking more detailed information about current federal law can find it in the ATF publication, *Federal Firearms Regulation Reference Guide* [ATF-P-5300.4 (10-95)].

Highlights of Federal Law

WAR REVENUE ACT, 1919. Government tax on firearms.

Although its purpose was to raise money to retire debts from World War I, the act established the precedent for the Treasury Department to have jurisdiction over firearms, and for an excise tax on firearms.

FIREARMS IN U.S. MAILS, 1927. Banned interstate mailing through the U.S. Postal Service of concealable firearms to individuals.

The purpose of this law was to prevent people living in areas with stricter firearm laws from circumventing local law by ordering guns by mail from areas with less restrictive laws. The law did not address shipping by means other than U.S. mail, so it was easily circumvented.

NATIONAL FIREARMS ACT, 1934. Regulated the sale of fully automatic weapons, silencers, sawed-off shotguns, belt-buckle guns, and others. The law also established a minimum barrel length for rifles and shotguns and prohibited their altering to make them easier to conceal (sawed-off shotguns).

The National Firearms Act essentially stopped widespread civilian use of the regulated weapons. The application process for purchasing an automatic weapon included: $200 transfer tax (an amount unchanged since), photograph, fingerprints, local police approval with four- to six-month waiting period, and background check. Early versions of the bill included a $1 transfer tax for handguns, but this was not enacted in the final version.[3]

GUN CONTROL ACT, 1968. Enabled ATF to establish rules and fees for Federal Firearm Licenses for dealers, manufacturers, and importers, and to develop Factoring Criteria to ensure that imported weapons were for sporting purposes. It banned interstate sales and shipments to individuals of handguns, long guns, and ammunition (except to those in contiguous states where the laws of both states were followed) and established eighteen as the minimum age to purchase a long gun and twenty-one for a handgun from a licensed dealer. It required dealers to keep detailed records of incoming and outgoing guns.

This law was passed in the wake of the political assassinations of Martin Luther King, Jr. and Robert Kennedy. The Factoring Criteria to establish a sporting purpose for handguns included a minimum barrel length of three inches for revolvers and a minimum overall length of six inches for pistols, as well as giving points for high quality of design and materials, thus disallowing "Saturday Night Specials" for import. However, some manufacturers legally imported firearm parts to assemble in this country even though the assembled guns would not have passed the Factoring Criteria if imported.

FIREARM OWNERS PROTECTION ACT, and other gun legislation, 1986. This act legalized interstate sale of long guns if the seller and the purchaser follow laws of both states and the sale is made in person. Some rules for Federal Firearms Licenses were changed to reduce punishment for violations and curtail inspections by ATF. It restored some gun ownership rights to felons under appeal, and gave private owners more leeway to sell their guns without acquiring beforehand a dealer's license. It banned further manufacture of automatic weapons and importation of barrels for small handguns. It eliminated the earlier requirement that gun dealers keep records on ammunition sales and barred any agency from collecting dealer records into a central data source. The act repealed the Gun Control Act's ban on interstate and mail-order sales of ammunition. Later in 1986, legislation was passed that banned manufacture of ammunition made completely of specific hard metals because they could pierce soft body armor, but did not include bullets coated with these metals even though these can still pierce body armor.[3]

THE UNDETECTABLE FIREARMS ACT, 1988. Required "plastic" guns to trigger metal detectors or be visible by x-ray.

Following much press attention of the plastic guns, this law was enacted to ban firearms which would escape security measures such as metal detectors and x-rays at airports.

THE BRADY HANDGUN VIOLENCE PREVENTION ACT, 1993. The "Brady Law" requires a maximum five-day waiting period for purchase of a handgun so that a criminal background check can take place. It increased the fee for a Federal Firearms License from $30 to $200, and included provisions that make stealing guns from dealers a federal offense. The waiting period is required to end in 1999, when a national criminal background checking system is supposed to be in place.

Passing this law was for years the primary campaign of the organization Handgun Control, Inc. The law was named for James Brady, the press secretary of Ronald Reagan, who was injured with a handgun during a failed 1981 assassination attempt. The bill's five-day waiting period and background check were the subject of a long and hard-fought battle that some believe was of more symbolic than practical importance.[3] States that have their own laws requiring a criminal background check prior to the purchase of a handgun are not subject to the Brady Law's waiting provision. The increased Federal Firearms License fee have resulted in fewer applicants. The provisions making gun theft a federal offense may help make stolen weapons more scarce in illegal gun markets.

VIOLENT CRIME CONTROL AND LAW ENFORCEMENT ACT, 1994. (Also called the Assault Weapon Ban) Bans manufacture (not sale) of ammunition magazines that hold more than ten rounds and bans

Highlights of Federal Law

manufacture and sale of semiautomatic rifles and handguns ("assault weapons") with other specific characteristics.

The law says that ammunition magazines for semiautomatic firearms cannot hold more than ten rounds and that weapons for the civilian market cannot be manufactured with certain combinations of features such as folding stocks, pistol grips, bayonet mounts, threaded barrels for flash suppressors, barrel shrouds, or grenade launch mounts. It banned 19 firearms by name and covers a total of 184 models. It also covers new firearms with the characteristics listed above, but does not affect guns currently owned by U.S. citizens. At least one manufacturer is said to be equipping newly manufactured guns with high-capacity magazines that were reportedly manufactured prior to the law's passage.[4]

Public Health Implication: Federal firearm regulation demonstrates that efforts to restrict certain weapons in the civilian population can work. Automatic weapons, sawed-off shotguns, and imported Saturday Night Specials, while still in use in small numbers, are not current public health problems. While this ad hoc approach to federal legislation has had some effect, it would be useful to give federal agencies the rule-making authority needed to also deal with the unintended consequences of the laws, such as the rise of the domestic Saturday Night Special industry described in the previous chapter, or to monitor emerging technologies. Federal laws have addressed homicides and assaultive firearm injuries, not suicide and unintentional injuries. This reflects a criminal justice rather than public health perspective. Federal agencies with rule-making authority could begin to address product modifications that might reduce these other firearm deaths which are the majority (See Figure 1.2, Chapter 1).

State Regulations

States have the power to protect the safety and health of their citizens through the "police powers" that are reserved to the states by the United States Constitution.[1] Each state has a broad array of public health laws and regulations in place to prevent injury and disease. While one state's laws cannot change the policies of other states, they can serve as a model to be implemented by the nation or by other states.[5] Some states required automobile seat belts before federal implementation, for example.

Some laws and regulations affecting firearms common to several states include: state licensing of firearm dealers; prohibition of openly carrying of weapons; requirement of a permit to carry concealed weapons; requirement to wait a certain time prior to purchasing a gun (before the implementation of the federal waiting period); requirement of a license to purchase and carry handguns; and the prohibition of sales of assault weapons (prior to federal law).

State law often differentiates handguns and long guns. One state, Maryland, has established a Handgun Roster Board that maintains a roster of guns that are allowed for manufacture and possession. Guns not on the roster, such as Saturday Night Specials, cannot be manufactured or sold in the state.[6] Washington, D.C. has banned the possession of all handguns not owned and registered prior to 1976.[7] In 1993, Virginia, a state which had relatively lax gun sale laws, limited sales of handguns to one per person per month in an attempt to stop the purchase of guns in Virginia for illegal resale in other locales, including Washington, D.C. This law was successful in reducing the dominance of Virginia in this illegal market. Unfortunately it appears that other states took up the slack.[8]

Meanwhile, other states are passing laws that make access to guns easier. Many states have loosened restrictions on carrying concealed weapons.[9] Texas passed such a law in 1995 so that, for the first time since 1857, an individual can easily get a permit to carry a concealed handgun. The provisions require that an individual obtain a permit ($140), be eligible to purchase a weapon under federal law, and take a fifteen-hour class in proper use of the weapon and in conflict resolution.[10]

Public Health Implication: State laws tend to address the sale, distribution, and use of firearms, not product design. With other consumer products, such as motor vehicles, or home hot-water heaters, action by several states which required manufacturers to change their products resulted in industry-wide voluntary changes that affected the manufacturers nationwide.[5] This included the requirement that seat belts be installed in cars—a change actively resisted by automobile manufacturers forty years ago.[11]

State Regulations

States can delegate authority to protect the public's health and safety to local municipalities and have done so under "home rule" provisions that typically address such things as building codes and zoning laws.[12] Many local ordinances pertaining to firearms are "hold and carry" laws that affect under what circumstance a firearm can be used. However, in 1981, Morton Grove, Illinois, passed an ordinance that banned possession of handguns. Shortly thereafter, the National Rifle Association started a campaign to pass so-called "preemption" laws for firearms in each state. Their reason was to combat restrictive local ordinances, which were becoming popular.[3, 13]

Preemption is a tricky concept, but Jon Vernick, gun policy legal expert, summarizes it clearly:

> Local laws can be preempted in two different ways—either expressly or implicitly. Express preemption occurs when a state law or a provision of the state constitution specifically prohibits localities from regulation in a particular area. . . . Implied preemption occurs when the body of the state laws within a given subject matter (like the regulation of guns) suggests an intention by the state legislature to occupy the field of regulation in that subject to the exclusion of local laws.[13]

When the state has preempted gun laws, localities either may not be allowed to establish local ordinances more restrictive than state laws or, in some cases, may not have any local ordinances at all relating to firearms. In Wisconsin, for example, a preemption law was passed in 1995. It made null and void the following local ordinances in cities and towns throughout the state:

> A twenty-year-old law prohibiting sale of handguns in Madison, Wisconsin; a newer law in Madison prohibiting possession of semiautomatic rifles and fragmenting ammunition and requiring that handguns be encased and unloaded while in transport; city ordinances throughout Wisconsin prohibiting the open carrying of weapons; city ordinances that prohibit the discharge of weapons within city limits; city ordinances that prohibit the window

rying of uncased and loaded weapons.[14]

More than forty states preempt most or all local gun laws. Passing these laws has been a well-acknowledged political goal of the National Rifle Association for the past decade.

Public Health Implication: Some urban areas, reflecting their higher rates of firearm injury and death, adopted more stringent firearms requirements than were in effect in rural areas. For states with preemptive laws, this avenue of changing gun policies may no longer be open, depending on the definition and scope of preemption in their state.[13] A set of federal laws that address the public health impact of firearms may preempt both state and local laws. Federal initiatives that involve design and performance standards for products sold throughout the country may be more effective than state-by-state regulation, but, paradoxically, may come about because of state actions.[5]

Many public health initiatives involve changes that affect vested economic interests, such as those of the tobacco industry, the automotive industry, and the alcoholic beverage industry. Firearm manufacturers and the groups they support are active in this discussion as well. Our democracy exists with an economy based on market forces and driven by profits, so that it requires continuous discussion and debate among members of a well-informed public to balance public health and private interests.

Voluntary Actions by Industry

While governmental regulation requires action according to law, industry can improve products and change marketing strategies voluntarily. Sometimes this occurs in response to adverse publicity. Following a spate of news articles and editorials, and New York Senator Daniel Moynihan's proposed *10,000 percent* federal excise tax, Winchester withdrew its "Black Talon" cartridge, which has a jacket that expands on impact into a razor-edged starburst (pictured in

Chapter 5).[15] Unfortunately, Winchester has resumed the manufacture and sale of this cartridge after slightly changing its design, and other manufacturers also produce controlled expansion bullets of varying designs.

For some products, there are industry associations that set voluntary standards. They do so to improve manufacturing efficiency and effectiveness; they may protect consumers as well. The Society of Automotive Engineers, for example, established standards for signal lights, brake lights, bumper heights, etc., which were followed voluntarily before the National Highway Traffic Safety Administration set up the Federal Motor Vehicle Safety Standards in the late 1960s and thereafter.

For firearms, however, there is much less activity. The Sporting Arms and Ammunition Manufacturing Institute sets standards for sizes of ammunition and has established voluntary performance standards for some firearm designs under conditions of abusive handling.[16]

Public Health Implication: Voluntary standards might prevent gun design variations that have a potential *negative* effect on user safety—cylinder rotation on revolvers, and, on semiautomatic pistols, thumb safety operations that vary from gun to gun, for example, because variations mean that knowing how to shoot one model of gun does not necessarily translate to knowing about all guns. With other potentially hazardous products, standards in design and operation have lowered rates of unintentional injury and death. Voluntary standard setting and voluntary action by manufacturers are important options that might be explored to help find common ground in promoting safer firearms. Sometimes if voluntary standards are not likely to be followed by all competitors, industries welcome federally mandated standards to "level the playing field."

Voluntary Actions by Industry

8

Strategies for Reducing Deaths and Injuries from Firearms

"It's too big a problem."
"Nothing we do can make a difference."
"It's so depressing, there's nothing anyone can do."

It is true that deaths and injuries from guns are an enormous problem in the United States. But, as with other big problems in our industrialized corporate economy, it is a problem that humans created and one they can creatively solve.

The problem can be solved by changing the guns themselves, by reducing the easy availability of most guns in our society, and by changing the incentives to use guns. One of the messages in this chapter is that there are a variety of solutions being proposed.

Because the "gun problem" is so big and so varied, there is no panacea—no one, single solution that will make everything all right. Public health advocates and others must try many different methods and push to have them evaluated carefully, so we know what works and why, and what doesn't work and should not be tried again.

Part of our strategy is to expand the narrow focus on "gun control"—keeping guns away from criminals—to include other approaches based on the science of injury control. One part of this strategy is considering the gun as a consumer product. Another is to focus intervention on high-risk populations, high-risk situations, and on the kinds of weapons that increase the probability of injury or death.

Our training is based on work with other hazardous products such as motor vehicles. We know that great results in reducing injuries and deaths can be achieved if changes are made to the product or if access to the product is reduced. Least effective in impact on the population is trying to change how individuals use the product. From our work with motor vehicles we know that death rates from frontal collisions are more likely to go down from having airbags in cars than from laws that require seat belt use. We also know, though, that in the absence of airbags, laws requiring seat belt use were more effective than relying on individuals to voluntarily buckle up each time they drove. A prerequisite to any seat belt use, of course, was requiring that manufacturers equip cars with seat belts, which was not routinely done until the mid-1960s.[1]

Changing the behavior of individuals solely through education is hard work. Even successful education programs may not be effective since people must take proper action each time they handle a gun if they are to protect themselves and their families. Changing the behavior of firearms manufacturers is also hard work and may not be accomplished without federal mandate. However, once it is done, it is effective because the products will be changed before they reach civilian hands.

Although our view is controversial, we believe that to reduce injuries and deaths society has to limit the availability of most guns and ammunition. This might be accomplished through raising prices or increasing taxes at the time of manufacture or sale, or by changing legal sales practices and disrupting illegal ones. It might be accomplished through changing incentives to have and use guns. We also must end easy access to guns at moments when impetuous action can result in deaths. This means addressing the ease with which people can carry guns on their persons and the incentives for keeping them easily available at home.

Fundamentally, our injury control training teaches us the fallacy of the slogan, "Guns don't kill people, people kill people." As Professor Susan Baker said, "People with guns *kill* people, people without guns *injure* people."[2] Other forms of interpersonal violence are much less likely to be lethal than firearms.

How Can Changes Be Accomplished?

For other injury problems facing our country, change has occurred through a mix of strategies. No single strategy solves all problems. Examples of social decisions about other products can guide us in our efforts to solve our gun problems. As a society, we have already tackled parts of the gun problem through the laws, regulations, and litigation. Examples of social decisions for other products can also guide us.

There are laws that established grenade launchers as "destructive devices," for example. Enforcement of this law means that our national firearms problems do not include the widespread availability and use of grenades by civilians. Only certain manufacturers can legally produce them and only the military can buy and use them. Regulation also resulted in a tax on automatic weapons and mandatory procurement procedures that have drastically reduced possession of these weapons. If we can determine that some weapons are clearly problematic and deserving of severe restrictions, then through careful study we can come up with appropriate restrictions for other obviously dangerous weapons.

Product Liability Litigation

Litigation or its threat can change the economic incentives that drive manufacturers and dealers. When laws and regulation have not successfully protected people from hazardous products, some people turn to product liability suits. These are decided by courts which may be less susceptible to the intense lobbying that usually surrounds legislative and regulatory processes when a product's hazard is under discussion.[3] Product liability suits, or their threat, have eliminated some injury hazards from many consumer products including passenger cars.[3] They were instrumental in the eventual inclusion in passenger cars of air bags and other passive restraint systems that have reduced death and injury by thousands in recent years. Currently, some activists are seeking to use this approach to effect similarly important changes in the design and manufacturing of firearms.

For cars, until the late 1960s, the rule of law was that manufacturers were not expected to produce cars that did anything more than provide transportation.[3] There were no successful product liability suits or appeals of judgments denying damages for crash injuries when these were based on a theory of vehicle crashworthiness.[3] Then, an article by Ralph Nader and Joseph Page appeared in the *Journal of the American Trial Lawyers Association*. It encouraged trial lawyers to use product liability laws to pressure automotive manufacturers to improve their products' crashworthiness.[3] They said, "The judicial process would seem to be an effective instrument for shifting to the automobile industry the cost of accidents caused by unsafe design."[3] Eventually, in 1968, an appeals court ruled that a car needed to provide as *safe* transportation as current technology and design allowed. With this ruling as precedent, product liability suits became increasingly successful and increasingly bothersome to the automotive industry. To avoid the costs of damages won in successful suits and the attendant bad publicity, motor vehicle manufacturers designed their products differently.[3]

There have been some successful product liability suits for firearms. A well-known one, *Kelley v. RG Industries*, involved a man shot in a robbery with a small, cheap revolver, a Saturday Night Special, manufactured by RG Industries.[3, 4] The suit argued that this kind of gun was commonly used in similar crimes, and either the manufacturer knew, or should have known that one of its weapons was likely to be used this way. This suit was won on appeal in the highest court of Maryland. The manufacturer was no longer able to obtain liability insurance and stopped producing this kind of weapon in the United States.[3, 5] RG Industries was the fifth largest producer of handguns of this kind when it stopped making them.[4]

Unlike motor vehicles, however, this case did not go on to be the harbinger of change for others manufacturing Saturday Night Specials. Instead, when Maryland passed the legislation that led to the Handgun Roster Board, described previously, the legislature also passed a law that said, "A person or entity may not be held liable for damages of any kind resulting from injuries sustained as a result of the criminal use of any firearm by a third person...," thus preventing similar suits from being successful in Maryland.[3] Other courts in other states have rejected the reasoning applied in *Kelley v. RG Industries*.[5]

But other product liability suits regarding firearms employing different legal theories continue around the country. One suit has been filed against the company Beretta on behalf of the parents of a teenager shot and killed by a friend. The friend had removed the magazine from a Beretta 9 mm semiautomatic and thought that it therefore was not loaded. But the gun had a cartridge in the chamber which discharged when the friend pulled the trigger. The suit maintains that Beretta should have been able to manufacture the gun so that it could not be used by an unauthorized person and, also, that Beretta should have designed the gun so that an inexperienced user would have been able to determine that it was loaded.[4]

Another suit is being filed on behalf of victims of multiple homicides in an office building in San Francisco.[5] In this case, the assailant

Product Liability Litigation

used two TEC-DC9 assault pistols equipped with "Hell-Fire" trigger accelerators that allow the shooter to fire more quickly. Manufacturers of both the TEC-DC9 and the trigger accelerators are defendants in the suit. This suit maintains, in part, that the manufacturers should be held responsible when they sell to the general public firearms and related products that are "especially well suited for mass destruction and ill-suited for legitimate sporting or self-defense use."[6] This suit is proceeding to trial following a ruling by a Superior Court judge in California that a manufacturer of assault weapons may be held accountable for damages resulting from criminal misuse of the product.[6]

It is not yet possible to tell whether product liability suits filed against gun manufacturers will be as successful in preventing injuries and deaths as were those filed against motor vehicle manufacturers over the past thirty years. But this approach is one of many that is being pursued to reduce the risks of firearm injuries and deaths.

Public Health Implication: In product liability suits such as these, plaintiffs seek not only economic compensation but also to establish legal precedents that other persons, similarly harmed, can use. Often, when the legal precedents, adverse publicity, or economic costs get to be bad enough, manufacturers will change the design of the product and its manufacture. The cap on punitive damages for product liability suits that was passed by the 104th Congress in 1996 and eventually vetoed by President Clinton might have made this approach to injury control less useful.

Marketing and Education

Marketing strategies by the firearm industry increased handguns sales after a sales slump in the early 1980s. Marketing strategies can be equally well employed to market safer guns or less lethal forms of self-protection, or to educate people on the real problems with guns kept in the home. For passenger cars, for example, safety features such as airbags and antilock brakes are now widely promoted in advertisements. But this fairly recent phenomenon was preceded by years of active industry resistance that "safety won't sell." It took federal regulation coupled with litigation for the manufacturers to include many safety features.[1]

Engineering has led to remarkable developments in accuracy, rates of fire, and power in firearm and ammunition technology. Engineering has also produced nonlethal ammunition and guns which cannot be fired by unauthorized users.

Some organizations working to change current public policies that affect firearms are listed in Appendix 3. While we do not necessarily endorse all of the efforts that each promotes, they are there for you as additional sources of information.

Changing the Gun and the Ammunition

One strategy widely used in injury control is to change the product design or to add features that reduce the probability of injury and death. Many technologies have already been developed, which, if made standard features on guns and ammunition, would reduce the possibility of injury and death. What follow are, for the most part, examples of existing technology that should be part of the public discussion on guns.

Safety Devices for Firearms

While some guns have safety devices, there are no regulations that require them, nor are there standards for their design. As we pointed out in Chapter 3, some thumb safeties, for example, are activated when the lever is in an "up" position, others when it is "down." Safety devices have mostly been developed to prevent accidental discharge when the gun is dropped or snagged on clothing, but some devices have also been developed to prevent unintentional use. Some newer pistols come without any user operated safeties at all. Few safety devices have been designed specifically to prevent a child's use of a gun, although many are needed and some currently produced devices could be altered to "childproof" the gun.

Many safety devices already available on revolvers and semiautomatic pistols were designed in the early twentieth century to prevent accidental discharge if the gun were jarred or dropped. These include:

TRANSFER BARS. In Chapter 3 we discussed the problem of accidental discharge with single action revolvers where the hammer rests on the firing pin and can jar it into shooting if dropped. Revolvers with transfer bars are designed with a gap between the firing pin and the hammer so the gun cannot be discharged unless the transfer bar bridges the gap, which happens when the shooter fully cocks the firearm (See Figure 3.2, and 3.3).

GRIP SAFETIES. These have been available on some semiautomatic pistols for many years and on revolvers in the past. (Figure 3.4) This device on the gun grip allows the weapon to be fired only if it is pushed in, as it would be if the gun were being held to be fired. This is similar in concept to the railroad locomotive's "dead man's throttle," which was designed to require positive pressure on the throttle or the engines would stop. The grip safety was designed in 1884 by the son of D.B. Wesson, one of the founders of Smith & Wesson. According to the story, D.B. Wesson heard of a child who was injured while shooting a handgun and commissioned a childproof design from his son. The grip safety was manufactured on models of Smith & Wesson guns from 1888 to 1937 and marketed as a childproof feature because a child's hand was too small and weak to pull the trigger and hold the grip safety down at the same time. The grip safety was discontinued when Smith & Wesson changed its manufacturing strategy and started producing weapons for the British military in 1937.[4] Steve Teret, of The Johns Hopkins Center for Gun Policy and Research, points out that the LadySmith, Smith & Wesson's small gun designed especially for women, does not come equipped with a grip safety even though small children often share living space with women.[4]

MANUAL THUMB SAFETIES. Perhaps the most common safety device is a lever that is either pushed up or down, depending on the weapon. When it is engaged, the gun cannot be fired. Obviously, without an industry standard as to what the positions mean, these safeties can be confusing to the shooter who does not have training or familiarity with the gun.

Technologies have also been developed to keep unauthorized users from firing weapons. This has great potential in childproofing guns and in keeping them from being used by angry or suicidal adolescents. It would also deter theft because the gun cannot be readily fired by any but an authorized user.

Safety Devices

TRIGGER LOCKS. Trigger locks can be purchased at gun supply stores. When a gun owner fastens a trigger lock to the trigger guard, the lock keeps the trigger from being pulled. The lock has to be put on or removed each time a person wants others to be prevented from using the gun, which is somewhat bothersome and therefore may not be done consistently.

COMBINATION LOCKS. The pistol in Figure 8.1 has a combination lock which has been retrofitted by a gunsmith. The technology of this safety device differs from a trigger lock because it is an integral part of the gun and does not need to be installed each time it is used, thus increasing the likelihood that it will be used. Retrofitting, however, requires a special effort and expense by the owner. Therefore, it may not be done by a large number of gun purchasers.

ELECTROMAGNETIC LOCKS. One manufacturer, Fulton Arms, advertises a .357 Magnum revolver with a three-part personalization feature: an electromagnetic encoder that establishes a frequency and is small enough to fit into a finger ring, an electromagnetic decoder embedded in the grip of the revolver, and a custom-fitted grip to ensure that the encoder and decoder come into line. The gun cannot be fired until the electromagnetic lock is unlocked, as would happen when the authorized user, wearing the encoder ring, gripped the revolver handle. Colt Manufacturing Company has a .40 caliber semiautomatic pistol in the prototype testing stage that also employs a radio frequency technology and a transponder worn by the user. It is supposed to be available in several years.

OTHER PERSONALIZATION DEVICES. Palm print, finger print, or voice activated personalization devices have also been suggested and have been used in other settings for security purposes.

Public Health Implication: Devices which require more active intervention by the user are likely to be less effective in lowering injury rates. For example, using a trigger lock requires several actions: purchasing the lock, installing it on the gun, removing it for each use, and reinstalling it. A personalized gun requires only purchasing and fitting; no action is required to keep the gun from discharging unintentionally.

Safety Devices

LOADED-CHAMBER INDICATORS. "I didn't know it was loaded" is one of the things said after unintentional shootings. Many medical examiners classify events such as these as homicides even though the legal system may characterize them slightly differently. Loaded-chamber indicators indicate that there is a round in the firing chamber. Not all guns have indicators, and, on those that do, they are often subtle and difficult to recognize for someone who is not familiar with the gun. An easily recognizable loaded-chamber indicator as standard equipment on all guns would be useful. Figure 4.1 depicts a loaded-chamber indicator.

MAGAZINE SAFETIES. A magazine safety prevents a pistol from being fired if the magazine is removed, even though there might still be a cartridge in the firing chamber. Inexperienced users, who are most often associated with deaths and injuries from unintentional discharge, may not realize that removing the magazine from a pistol does not completely "unload" a weapon if a cartridge has already been fed from the magazine into the chamber. Although some semiautomatic pistols

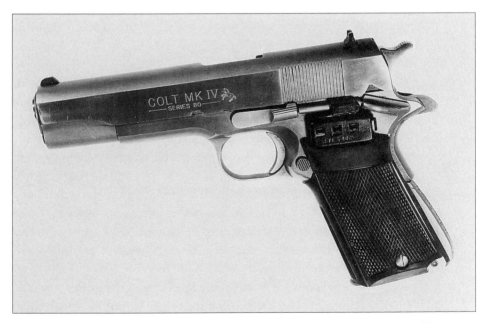

FIGURE 8.1 ONE TYPE OF TRIGGER LOCK. The lock can be seen above the grip. There are three buttons which have to be pressed in a specific order to unlock the trigger. This lock has been retrofitted by a gunsmith.

Safety Devices

come equipped with magazine safeties, they are not required on all semiautomatic pistols manufactured and sold in the United States.

Unfortunately, guns that are equipped with magazine safeties are associated with several deaths each year that occur when the shooter inserts an empty magazine into the gun but the chamber already contains a live cartridge. An inexperienced user points the gun at someone and pulls the trigger, not realizing that the weapon is loaded. The cartridge remaining in the chamber is then discharged.

Public Health Implication: Every year children and adolescents are killed when they are accidentally shot by other children.[7] If guns are kept in the house, it is pertinent to think about devices to prevent a child from firing a gun. The personalization devices described above might be the most useful and easily applied technology. Another suggestion has been to require a grip safety that is too big and strong for a child to activate while pulling the trigger. The Government Accounting Office determined that childproof safety devices and loaded-chamber indicators would reduce the number of unintentional firearm deaths by 30 percent—about four hundred and fifty deaths per year.[8]

Reducing Ease of Concealment

Easily concealed weapons have been a social concern for some time. The National Firearms Act of 1934 expressly prohibited the altering of rifles and shotguns to make them easier to conceal. The Gun Control Act of 1968 established minimum lengths for handguns for import into the U.S. in an effort to reduce concealable weapons. Laws in some states treat concealed weapons stringently, prohibiting the carrying of a concealed weapon entirely or requiring special permission from law enforcement agents to do so. There is a trend in states, however, to ease restrictions against carrying concealed weapons, and in many, state law *requires* legal authorities to issue permits to citizens who are legally able to purchase weapons.[9]

Concealed weapons are immediately accessible to the carrier and can be easily carried into high-risk situations such as taverns or potential robbery sites. Because the gun is not visible, bystanders have no opportunity to escape a dangerous situation, nor do law enforcement agents know to intervene. Barrel length is an excellent measure of concealability.

The barrel length of the weapon depicted in Figure 6.5 is about 2.5 inches. The gun can be carried in a pants or coat pocket without being noticed. Firearms with barrel lengths this short cannot be fired accurately beyond about six yards.

In Milwaukee more than 75 percent of the handguns associated with homicides involved short-barreled weapons.[10] Police reports of weapons confiscated and destroyed show large proportions are short-barreled handguns.[11]

The largest manufacturers of small-barreled handguns lead the industry in handgun production.[11] Requiring that domestic guns meet the same criteria as foreign imports would be one way to increase average barrel length in the U.S. gun stock.

Concealability could also be addressed by improving our ability to detect hidden guns. Remote sensors have been developed that would allow law enforcement officers to "scan" a person for hidden firearms from a safe distance.

Public Health Implication: Concealed weapons are related to deaths from homicides rather than suicide or unintentional injury. Many homicides occur not in criminal contexts but as outcomes of alcohol-fueled disputes among friends and families. A readily available gun can mean that some arguments will have a lethal outcome. Homicides and assaultive injuries occurring in robberies or other criminal behavior are also made easier with concealed weapons.

Improving the Quality of Guns Manufactured

While the Factoring Criteria impose some quality standards on imported firearms—giving more points for weapons made with high-grade steel and safety devices—domestic manufacturers have no required quality standards. Some companies, notably the California companies related to the Jennings family (Phoenix Arms, Lorcin Engineering, Davis Industries, Sundance Industries, and Bryco Arms, formerly Jennings Arms), produce guns of low quality with unreliable loading mechanisms, components made of relatively soft metals, and few safety devices.[11, 12] (All of their guns go by the manufacturer's name, with the exception of the Raven, manufactured now by Phoenix Arms.) Consequently, the guns are very inexpensive to manufacture.

Industry experts consider these guns "junk" and routinely recommend against buying them.[11]

In January of 1997, the American Handgun Standards Act was introduced in Congress to require that domestic handguns follow the Factoring Criteria of ATF. Requiring more stringent quality standards for the domestic industry should effectively raise the price of weapons and reduce their availability.

Changing the Lethality of Guns and Ammunition

It is possible to restrict new technologies that would increase the lethality of the existing United States gun stock. It might also be possible to produce guns that serve both sporting purposes and self-protection, while at the same time reducing their lethality. Since guns and ammunition are designed to be lethal, consciously reducing their lethality may seem counterintuitive. But, in this society we often restrict technology that threatens public safety. For example, we have banned production of certain pesticides because of their potential damage. Balancing public health needs and private interests is a constant struggle in contemporary society.

MAGAZINE CAPACITY. Since it takes a bullet to make a wound, it follows that more bullets are likely to make more wounds, in one person or many. A mentally disturbed man killed six people and injured nineteen on the Long Island Railway in 1993 with four fifteen-round detachable magazines and a 9 mm Ruger.[13] Before the passage of the 1994 Violent Crime Control and Law Enforcement Act, there were no standards to limit the number of cartridges a magazine could contain. Since then, magazines that hold more than ten rounds cannot be manufactured for sale to the civilian population. Weapons that accept magazines with higher capacity can still be manufactured, and high-capacity magazines manufactured before 1994 can still be legally sold. The manufacturer of the TEC 9 is selling weapons with a thirty-two-round magazine. All gun parts are new except the magazines, which the company says were produced before 1994.[14]

In the wake of the 1994 Violent Crime Control and Law Enforcement Act, some manufacturers altered their weapons so as to be legal, but did not alter significantly the speed at which the weapon could be fired or change other features that might be of concern. For example, Figures 8.2 and 8.3 show how a semiautomatic rifle has been modified by the manufacturer to meet the current law: The pistol grip has been removed, but the stock has been modified so the firearm can still be gripped with one hand.

The current law restricting the manufacture of weapon magazines with a capacity greater than ten was considered for repeal by the 104th Congress elected in 1994. The effectiveness of the current law should be scientifically evaluated for the degree to which it has been enforced, the degree to which it has reduced the number and proportion of high-capacity weapons in the country, and its effect on criminal activity, and on the firearm death rate from homicides.

SPEED OF FIRING. A desire to increase the speed of fire has driven many technologic advances in firearms history. It produced the revolver, the semiautomatic pistol and rifle, and the automatic machine gun. Increasing the rate of fire means inflicting more wounds in a given period of time, again, either to one individual or many. Manufacture of automatic machine guns for civilian sale was halted in 1986, and their availability to the civilian population was curtailed by the 1934 National Firearms Act. Methods of reducing firing speeds in the guns of this country should be investigated.

FIGURE 8.2 ASSAULT WEAPON. This semiautomatic rifle has a pistol grip for easily shooting with one hand, an extended magazine holding about thirty rounds (a "banana clip"), and a folded bayonet. Prior to 1994 legislation, this gun was available to the civilian market. The manufacturer is Norinco, of Beijing, China.

Changing the Lethality of Guns

FIGURE 8.3 MODIFIED ASSAULT WEAPON. The same model of assault weapon pictured in Figure 8.2 has been modified to meet legal requirements of 1994 federal legislation on assault weapons. The magazine is smaller and holds no more than ten cartridges. The stock has been modified by Norinco, the manufacturer, to function like a pistol grip, and the bayonet has been removed. The magazine can easily be replaced with a higher capacity one that was made before 1994.

Public Health Implication: In the interest of thoroughly exploring options, we need to consider whether we can promote the use of single-shot weapons. While this seems impractical, William Haddon, Jr., M.D., a founder of modern injury control, always said to consider *every* option that might result in the prevention of injuries or the reduction of their severity. Sometimes, in considering options that seem unrealistic, new ideas are generated.

POWER. Especially disturbing is the increase in power among small, easily concealed handguns. No longer just .22 caliber revolvers, these weapons now include .380 caliber and 9 mm semiautomatic pistols.[11] Change is also evidenced by the increased use of larger caliber firearms in Milwaukee homicides over the five year period from 1990 to 1994. During that period, the proportion of homicide weapons that were 9 mm caliber grew from 7 percent to nearly 25 percent. The proportion of suicide firearms that were 9 mm caliber also grew from 0 percent in 1990 to 9 percent in 1994.[10]

Sometimes large-caliber, powerful weapons are difficult to use. They are heavy and their recoil is strong. Lighter materials and recoil compensators may make these weapons easier to use, and hence more attractive to some types of shooters.[15] If this is the case, we may begin to see more deaths and injuries from .45 and .50 caliber weapons.

Public Health Implication: The increasing power of the firearms in general circulation has forced law enforcement agencies to use higher powered weapons. By reducing the availability of high-powered weapons to the civilian population, we might stop this mini arms race. Following the example of the 1934 National Firearms Act, a transfer tax that goes up with the power of the weapon, its rate of fire, or its magazine capacity could be levied. An increased tax might deter the casual purchaser and lead to a decrease in high-powered weapons in the U.S. gun supply.

ACCURACY. The short barrel length of a handgun makes accurate shooting difficult. A handgun with a barrel length of less than four inches cannot reliably place a bullet at its point of aim if the target is more than about twenty-five feet away from the gun. Even though the majority of shootings occur at a range of seven yards or less, the shooter misses the intended victim most of the time. One study reported that even at close range, police only hit assailants they are shooting at 25 percent of the time, and assailants shooting at police only hit them 11 percent of the time.[16] Widespread use of laser aiming devices that make it easier for the shooter to aim could potentially increase the number of fatalities and injuries. This device can be integral or hand mounted, so that, when aimed, the laser beam appears as a red dot on the target. While the gun itself may not be accurate enough to place a bullet at the point of aim, the shooter no longer needs much skill to aim the weapon. Laser sights are available to civilians. Their use by civilians is not regulated by any government laws and they are outside the jurisdiction of the ATF.[15, 17] Current prices are less than $200.

Public Health Implication: Occasionally there is ample press attention for a new technology that seems particularly dangerous. This attention has led to legislation, as with armor-piercing bullets and plastic guns. But laser sights have not received this kind of press attention, and there is no public health authority to evaluate their likely effect on deaths and injuries from firearms. Stopping widespread use of laser sights may be important; it may prevent an increase in deaths and injuries, especially from assaults. Laser sights could be taxed or banned from sale to civilians.

Changing the Lethality of Guns

When law enforcement agents want to know about the gun used in a crime, forensic crime laboratories examine cartridge cases and other ballistic evidence. If caseless ammunition became widely used, law enforcement and other forensic specialists would lose an important tool. The technology for caseless ammunition has been developed but it is not in widespread use.[17, 18]

> **Public Health Implication:** Guns that use caseless ammunition are a relatively new technology that might be exploited in marketing to increase gun sales. Losing the ability to trace weapons through the cartridge cases would be a cause of concern to the criminal justice community. As with laser sight technology, preventing the dissemination of caseless ammunition early would be easier than trying to control it once it is in widespread use.

Ammunition

Any ammunition can be lethal if it strikes a vulnerable anatomic site, but some ammunition currently available for the civilian population is particularly likely to produce lethal wounds, for example, expanding bullets. Use of these forms of ammunition could be discouraged in the civilian population through regulation, litigation, taxation, or actions to reduce demand.

> **Public Health Implication:** We need more scientific research from a public health perspective to know the likely effect of decreasing usage of expanding and hollow-point bullets.

The "Glaser Safety Slug" has number 12 birdshot pellets embedded in a .357 Magnum cartridge which is sealed with a plastic cap.[16, 18] Because these projectiles decelerate rapidly and expend all of their energy near the surface of the body, they, like shotgun blasts, cause huge surface wounds and massive tissue destruction. These bullets were "twice as effective as the best hollow points, and five times as effective as non-hollow point" when measured on their ability to inflict tissue damage.[16] The trauma physician reporting about them to his colleagues in 1986 was grateful that the price of this ammunition was high enough to discourage widespread use.[16]

This trauma physician also points out that in the ballistic science conducted by ammunition manufacturers for the military there is a continuing emphasis on larger caliber bullets which can "punch out" more tissue, and on high-velocity, fragmenting, or hollow-point ammunition which maximizes energy release in the tissue, and thus tissue damage.[16] He goes on to say, "Unfortunately for medical science, this means larger, more complex wounds, and fewer successful resuscitations." This ammunition could be banned for sale to the civilian population or taxes could be levied on the purchaser or the manufacturer. High prices for ammunition having especially lethal characteristics might be a useful strategy to decrease use.

USE OF NONLETHAL AMMUNITION. In Ireland, Switzerland, and Israel, police weapons use very large caliber rubber bullets which can not penetrate skin.[18] In some European countries people also use bullets that are not lead or metal, but capsules of tear gas. They subdue the victim without inflicting penetrating wound injuries. Substituting less lethal forms of ammunition for what is currently available to United States civilians would seen eminently practical. Other nonpenetrating bullets include "stun bags" filled with a sandlike dust. These cause pain but do not penetrate the skin and are not likely to be lethal.[18] These weapons are similar to the electronic stun guns that police sometimes use to subdue suspects with temporary pain but without permanent injury. Interestingly, in this country, while anyone can buy a bullet that fragments and causes multiple wounds in the body, the sale of "gas" bullets is restricted to the military and law enforcement agents.

Changing Access to Firearms and Ammunition

United States residents have easier access to firearms and ammunition of every kind than residents of any other country in the world. Our death rates from firearms reflect this. The firearm homicide death rate is five times that of Scotland's, the second leading country for homicides. Just as differences in countries' diets result in differences in heart disease, stroke, and cancer, their different firearm death rates reflect different firearm availabilities.

Changing Access to Firearms

Many people cherish easy access to guns, however, and call efforts to modify this access "encroachments" on personal rights. But our society often chooses to balance private interests with social benefits. From a public health perspective, society can modify high death rates for firearms using a variety of means including changing current firearm access policies.

Making Handguns Harder to Get

Limiting access to handguns is not a new proposal. When the 1934 National Firearms Act was being developed, Saturday Night Specials were on the list of "gangster weapons," along with sawed-off shotguns, silencers, and automatic machine guns, to be tightly restricted in the civilian population.[17] And, similarly, in 1968, the Factoring Criteria for imported weapons were considered for application to all handguns sold in the United States.[11] In Washington, D.C., which has a very restrictive ban on handguns, homicides and suicides from handguns decreased from 1977 to 1988, even though handguns were easily available outside the city limits. And there was no increase in homicides by other means that compensated for the decrease of gun-related homicides.[19] Barriers to purchase can be effective deterrents to homicides and suicides. Although the approach is politically challenging, handgun availability, especially Saturday Night Specials, might be cut by mandating quality standards for design and manufacture, adding excise taxes to handguns in inverse proportion to their barrel lengths, and creating criteria for special taxes or for restricting sale on select handguns.

Improving Sales Monitoring and Disrupting Illegal Sales

Right now it is easy to obtain a federal firearms dealer's license, although it was much easier a few years ago. There are almost ten times as many licensees as there are members of the Stocking Gun Dealers Trade Association (150,000 compared to 16,000).[20] Our society could require that federal licensees be bona fide gun dealers in a retail establishment. Permitting kitchen table dealers makes it extremely difficult to enforce gun laws. The screening process for purchasers could be improved, and background checks could include looking for high-risk misdemeanors. Federal firearms licensees could be required to have adequate business liability insurance, and to store their wares in safe

places (much like requirements for pharmacies and narcotics). All
firearms transfers, including swaps, sales at gun shows and flea markets, could require the paperwork gun dealers must prepare. The purchaser's background would have to be checked for a criminal record. Illegal gun trafficking could be disrupted by requiring all states and municipalities to have similarly strict sales practices and ordinances. Law enforcement "buy and bust" operations to disrupt illegal street sales of guns should be encouraged. All of these could be accomplished through federal regulation and by increasing the enforcement capabilities of the Bureau of Alcohol, Tobacco, and Firearms.[21, 22]

Further Restricting Gun Ownership

Some states now restrict gun purchases by individuals under a restraining order for domestic abuse and give law enforcement agencies the right to confiscate weapons from these individuals. Requirements could be established for people who have large private arsenals of firearms. Law enforcement could be permitted to confiscate weapons temporarily or permanently for just cause. We could increase enforcement of gun laws in high-risk locations—taverns known to law enforcement because of brawls, for example. A high level of active, public enforcement of existing weapons laws has reduced gun incidents in some cities.[21, 22] Disrupting illegal markets for youth has been so successful in one city that a new federal program to trace guns confiscated in youth crimes has been introduced in seventeen cities across the nation.[23]

Changing Incentives to Have and Use Guns

How can the current social incentives to own and use guns be changed? A strategy might be to target the growing number of people who purchase guns for self-defense. For this group, it will be important to continue the research that measures the higher risk of homicide, suicide, and accidental death and injury when guns are kept in the home. Other, less lethal means of self-protection might allay the fears that otherwise motivate people to purchase guns, and if so, then promoting these means would be in order. Advertisements that promote guns for self-protection could be stopped, altered, or countered with "social marketing."

Some less lethal means of self-protection include pepper gas, rubber bullets, guard dogs, or electric security systems. Many criminologists suggest using community policing, which builds community through neighborhood watches, and active police involvement in the community. Merely decreasing the availability of guns on the street might also calm fears and reverse the spiral of citizens arming to protect themselves against armed criminals.

The changing public perception of smoking is a good analogy. Although smoking is not yet eradicated, the number of smokers in this country is decreasing yearly. This has been accomplished by public education campaigns, changes in advertising policies, sales restrictions, liability litigation, restriction on smoking in public places, and active clinical interventions by physicians and other practitioner groups. A similar effort may change the public perception of firearms and their utility.

Changing the Information Infrastructure

Information must be available to help legislators, researchers, policy makers, law enforcement officials, and citizens plan and evaluate policies, identify high-risk weapons, locales, and populations, and educate the public. We must systematically gather, analyze, and distribute information on the firearms involved in deaths and injuries, and on the circumstances, victims and assailants.

Similar information has been available for years on motor vehicle crashes through the federally funded Fatal Accident Reporting System (FARS). This system reports on the make, model, and vehicle type of fatal crashes in the United States. It includes information on drivers, passengers, circumstances of the crash, and use of protective devices. These data have been used widely to improve passenger vehicle safety by federal and state governments, public health and safety researchers, the insurance industry, and the automotive industry.

There is no similar national or state system for firearm deaths and injuries, and only recently has there been complete information for a locality.[10, 24, 25] The Centers for Disease Control and Prevention (CDC) helped initiate a handful of firearm injury surveillance systems for research and evaluation. However, many of them have no access to information on the make, model, and serial number of weapons involved in firearm injury and death. For firearm deaths, two national computer data bases supply some information. The U.S. Vital Records system has death certificate information from each state, and the FBI's Uniform Crime Report collects information for homicides from police departments. Neither is sufficient. Death certificates lack information on the assailant, the circumstances, or the weapon, even whether it was a handgun or long gun. The Uniform Crime Report has no information on suicides or unintentional deaths, and lacks specific information on the firearm used in homicides except to identify it as a handgun or long gun.

Weapons Owned in the Population

For information on motor vehicle crashes, high-risk situations, and high-risk populations, the states' files on licensed drivers and registered vehicles are almost as important as FARS data. These files give us baseline information about how many cars of a certain model and vintage are in use. By comparing data on fatal crashes from FARS to this baseline we can see which cars are disproportionately associated with deaths. We have no such information on firearms. Central registration on who owns guns would provide comparable baseline data, but many people profoundly distrust this approach. It may be more politically feasible at this time to estimate the information by probability surveys, as the National Crime Victimization Survey does.

Ammunition Used in Crimes

Current technology could "fingerprint" or mark each bullet as it is fired. This permits matching the gun and the bullet with a high degree of probability. Marking is done either with the firing pin or by an idiosyncrasy in the rifled bore. Bullet identification would be invaluable for law enforcement.

Scientific Research

One public health researcher has compared the intensity of debate about firearms to that which met the 1964 *Surgeon General's Report on Smoking and Health*.[26] Incremental changes in public perception of smoking and health that resulted from that report and others that followed were due to the increasing weight of scientific evidence. While

Weapons Owned in the Population

public health interest in and research on firearms and their risks has increased dramatically over the past ten years, it is still limited by a lack of funds and funding agencies.[27, 28]

The research which does go on occurs in a highly politicized arena. For example, in 1995, ten United States senators signed a letter calling for complete dissolution of the CDC's National Center for Injury Prevention and Control. This agency is one of the very few government funding sources for *any* injury research and it runs a small number of programs for firearms research. The motive for the letter was eliminating firearms research, a goal that is still prominent on the Congressional agenda for some. As this is being written, the House Appropriations Committee voted to reduce the budget of the Centers for Disease Control and Prevention by $2.6 million, the amount spent on firearms research.[29]

The limited amount of federal money available for firearms research in 1995 is an improvement over 1988.[30] Then, in a 1988 editorial entitled "Deaths and Injuries from Firearms: Who Cares?" researchers pointedly described the nineteen research grants awarded by the National Institutes of Health for diseases that had resulted in 17 illnesses and 9 deaths that year, compared to the complete lack of funding for any grants to study firearms despite 198,000 injuries and 33,000 deaths annually.[30]

AFTERWORD

How does policy change occur? Probably no one knows what would produce the kind of sea-change required to change guns and their availability as we have described here. Yet changes that affect public health do occur, as the changes in motor vehicle safety, smoking, dietary and exercise habits over the past generation have shown. The public health community is not of one mind about the best way to achieve change for guns. Some argue for grassroots organizing. Others argue for using the strength of the physician community to counsel patients about the hazard of keeping guns in the home or to take an active role in developing gun policy. Some are interested in behind-the-scenes legislative work in national and state capitols. Others want to focus on the media and violence in the media. Still others propose teaching conflict resolution in schools or on the streets.

The lack of agreement about how to achieve change should not be surprising because the issues are very complex. And there is no single best approach. Effective, long-lasting change will result from action on all of these fronts as well as others.

We see signs that our collective efforts are beginning to pay off. Something is clearly changing in the medical and public health communities. Prestigious journals such as the *New England Journal of Medicine* and the *Journal of the American Medical Association* routinely publish articles about firearms, including risks associated with ownership, and trends in manufacturing. There is a growing body of scientific literature about guns and several journals have devoted complete issues to addressing parts of the problem. The *American Journal of Preventive Medicine* and *Health Affairs* are two examples.

Federal agencies, state and local health departments, and philanthropic foundations are beginning to fund research, surveillance, and prevention projects.

Citizen groups are forming and connecting to national organizations that promote activities to bring the problem to public attention or to seek changing laws and government policies.

Books like ours are being written to inform the growing number of people who see the need for change.

How long will it take? In our country, it seems that public health policy change occurs incrementally and over long periods of time. *The Surgeon General's Report on Smoking and Health* was released in 1964 and was based in part on definitive epidemiologic studies published in the early 1950s. It contained incontrovertible evidence that smoking was behind the increasing rates of lung cancer in the United States. Today, our society is still struggling with the proper role of the federal government and the FDA in the regulation of tobacco products, and although smoking rates have decreased among adults, they are rising among teenagers.

Airbags in cars are another example. The technology for airbags was first patented in 1952. The bags were installed on ten thousand General Motor cars in 1974 and functioned well. The Federal Department of Transportation first ordered airbags on 1974 model cars, amended the order to include automatic seat belts, rescinded it completely in 1974, reinstated it in 1977, rescinded it again in 1981, was sued by insurers, and finally, under direction from the Supreme Court reinstated the standard in 1984 to begin in 1987.[1, 3] Many manufacturers initially chose to meet the standard with automatic belts. Dual airbags finally will be required on 100 percent of passenger cars in the 1998 model year, and 100 percent of light trucks a year later. Now the presence of airbags and other safety features in their cars are advertised by automobile manufacturers.

Similarly, factory-installed seat belts were first called for by physicians in the 1930s, were first installed as standard equipment in 1959 (on Volvos), and were not required for all passenger cars until 1968.[1]

These actions were fueled by public health activists, trial lawyers, insurers who were paying for health care costs, concerned citizens, surviving victims, legislators, government workers, and researchers. The story is the same in most public health arenas—a diverse cast of characters fights and wins many small battles that, over time, add up to effective change.

These lessons should encourage patience and diligence. The path of public health history, when it is written for firearm injuries, is likely to be long and rocky, full of setbacks and minor victories. Significant amounts of work in the areas of grassroots activity, electoral politicking, media attention, scientific research, product liability suits, and legislative lobbying will continue to fuel the engine of change with respect to the public's view of guns, the way manufacturers market and design guns, the way legislators make policy, and the deployment of government agency resources.

The message of this primer is that change is not impossible. We do not have all the answers, but our experience and training tells us that the goal of reducing firearm injuries and their economic, social, and personal costs is within reach.

Afterword

APPENDIX I

Factoring Criteria for Handguns

This appendix contains text from ATF Form 4950, which describes the Factoring Criteria for weapons. The minimum qualifying score for pistols is 75. The minimum qualifying score for revolvers is 45.

Table A.1 Factoring Criteria for Pistols

Pistol Prerequisites
1. The pistol must have a positive manually operated safety device.
2. The combined length and height must not be less than 10″ with the height (right angle measurement to barrel without magazine or extension) being at least 4″ and the length being at least 6″.

Individual Characteristics	*Point Value*
OVERALL LENGTH	
For each 1/4″ over 6″	1
FRAME CONSTRUCTION	
Investment Cast or Forged Steel	15
Investment Cast or Forged HTS Alloy	20
WEAPON WEIGHT WITH MAGAZINE (Unloaded)	
Per ounce	1
CALIBER	
.22 Short and .25 Auto	0
.22 LR and 7.65 mm to .380 Auto	3
9 mm Parabellum and over	10
SAFETY FEATURES	
Locked Breech Mechanism	5
Loaded-Chamber Indicator	5
Grip Safety	3
Magazine Safety	5
Firing Pin Block or Lock	10
MISCELLANEOUS EQUIPMENT	
External Hammer	2
Double Action	10
Drift Adjustable Target Sight	5
Click Adjustable Target Sight	10
Target Grips	5
Target Trigger	2

　　　　Table A.2 Factoring Criteria for Revolvers

Revolver Prerequisites

1. Must pass safety test. A Double-Action Revolver must have a safety feature which automatically (or in a Single-Action Revolver by manual operation) causes the hammer to retract to a point where the firing pin does not rest upon the primer of the cartridge. The safety device must withstand the impact of a weight equal to the weight of the revolver dropping from a distance of 36″ in a line parallel to the barrel upon the rear of the hammer spur, a total of five times.
2. Must have overall frame (with conventional grips) length (not diagonal) of 4.5″ minimum.
3. Must have a barrel length of at least 3″.

Individual Characteristics	*Point Value*
BARRELL LENGTH (Muzzle to Cylinder Face)	
Less than 4″	0
For each 1/4″ over 4″	1/2
FRAME CONSTRUCTION	
Investment Cast or Forged Steel	15
Investment Cast or Forged HTS Alloy	20
WEAPON WEIGHT (Unloaded)	
Per ounce	1
CALIBER	
.22 Short to .25 ACP	0
.22 LR and .30 to .38 S&W	3
.38 Special	4
.357 Magnum and Over	5
MISCELLANEOUS EQUIPMENT	
Adjustable Target Sights (Drift or Click)	5
Target Grips	5
Target Hammer and Target Trigger	5

ATF Form 4473 is a record of an over-the-counter firearms transaction. This appendix contains the text of the section that the buyer completes and is included here to demonstrate the questions that must be answered before the transaction can be executed.

Section A. Must be completed personally by transferee (buyer). Where transaction is a sale, this section must be completed by actual buyer.

1. Transferee's (Buyer's) Name (Last, First, Middle)
   Sex: Male or Female
2. Height
3. Weight
4. Race
5. Residence Address (No., Street, City, County, State, ZIP Code)
6. Date of Birth (MM DD YY)
7. Place of Birth (City, State, or Foreign Country)
8. Certification of Transferee (Buyer). An untruthful answer may subject you to criminal prosecution. Each question must be answered with a "yes" or a "no" inserted in the box at the right of the question:
   a. Are you under indictment or information (a formal accusation of a crime made by a prosecuting attorney, as distinguished from an indictment presented by a grand jury) in any court for a crime punishable by imprisonment for a term exceeding one year?
   b. Have you been convicted in any court of a crime punishable by imprisonment for a term exceeding one year? (NOTE: A "yes" answer is necessary if the judge could have given a sentence of more than one year. A "yes" answer is not required if you have been pardoned for the crime or the conviction has been expunged or set aside, or you have had your civil rights restored and, under the law where the conviction occurred, you are not prohibited from receiving or possessing any firearm.)
   c. Are you a *fugitive* from justice?
   d. Are you an unlawful user of, or addicted to, marijuana, or any depressant, stimulant, or narcotic drug, or any other controlled substance?
   e. Have you ever been adjudicated mentally defective or have you been committed to a mental institution?
   f. Have you been discharged from the Armed Forces under *dishonorable* conditions?
   g. Are you an alien *illegally* in the United States?

h. Are you a person who, having been a citizen of the United States, has renounced his/her citizenship?

i. Are you subject to a court order restraining you from harassing, stalking, or threatening an intimate partner or child of such partner?

I hereby certify that the answers to the above are true and correct. If the transaction is a sale, I also certify that I am the actual buyer. I also understand that a person who answers "yes" to any of the above questions is prohibited from purchasing and/or possessing a firearm, except as otherwise provided by federal law. I also understand that the making of any false oral or written statement or the exhibiting of any false or misrepresented identification with respect to this transaction is a crime punishable as a felony.

Transferee's (Buyer's) Signature - execute at time of actual transfer of firearm(s)

Appendix 2

APPENDIX 3

A List of Concerned Organizations

The following organizations are active in advocacy and educational efforts related to firearm injuries. We include this information not as an endorsement of any specific organization or agenda, but as a source of information for interested readers.

Coalition to Stop Gun Violence
100 Maryland Avenue N.E. Suite 402
Washington, D.C. 20002

Educational Fund to End Handgun Violence
(Educational Arm of Coalition to Stop Gun Violence)
100 Maryland Avenue N.E. Suite 402
Washington, D.C. 20002

Handgun Control, Inc.
1225 Eye Street N.W.
Washington, D.C. 20005

The Center to Prevent Handgun Violence
1225 Eye St. N.W. Suite 1100
Washington, D.C. 20005
(Educational Arm of Handgun Control, Inc.)

HELP Network (Handgun Epidemic Lowering Plan)
Children's Memorial Medical Center
2300 Children's Plaza #88
Chicago, Illinois 60614

The Johns Hopkins University
Center for Gun Policy and Research
624 North Broadway
Baltimore, Maryland 21205

Violence Policy Center
1300 N. St. N.W.
Washington, D.C. 20005

APPENDIX 4

Where to Find Out More

Fact Sheets on firearm injuries and deaths are available at little or no cost from:

Children's Safety Network Clearinghouse
2070 Chain Bridge Road, Suite 450
Vienna, VA. 22182-2563
(703) 821-8955

Numbers and rates of death from firearms, as well as other references, can also be found easily if you have access to the Internet through a computer system, such as perhaps your local library might have. While most of the information about firearms is also available in a print publication, the Internet provides an easy means of access to the published material. United States Postal mailing addresses are included for the organizations listed here.

On the World Wide Web, the Centers for Disease Control and Prevention provides access to several important data sources where most of the mortality information for this book was found. Electronic addresses current at the time of publication are:

Centers for Disease Control and Prevention
http://www.cdc.gov

CDC WONDER Mortality Database
http://wonder.cdc.gov

Through the CDC WONDER computer system you can access a wide variety of information, including Monthly Vital Statistics Reports and Advance Data from the National Center for Health Statistics, and articles from the CDC's *Morbidity and Mortality Weekly Report* (*MMWR*). You can also write to the following address for back issues of the *MMWR*:

Editor, MMWR Series
Mailstop C-D8
Centers for Disease Control and Prevention
1600 Clifton Road, NE
Atlanta, Georgia 30333

Information on injuries from firearms is often reported first in the *Journal of the American Medical Association*. Abstracts of current articles can also be accessed through the Internet. Home page address:

> http://www.ama.assn.org
> Mailing address:
> American Medical Association
> 515 N. State Street
> Chicago, Illinois 60610

Other sources of bibliographic material, and other information, are:

> http://www.guninfo.org
> Mailing address:
> Harborview Injury Prevention and Research Center
> Box 359960
> 325 Ninth Avenue
> Seattle, Washington 98104-2499

> http://www.pcvp.org
> Mailing address:
> Pacific Center for Violence Prevention
> Trauma Foundation
> Building One, Room 300
> San Francisco General Hospital
> San Francisco, California 94110

Appendix 4

SOURCES

INTRODUCTION

1. Baker SP. Injury science comes of age. *Journal of the American Medical Association (JAMA)* 1989;262(16):2284.
2. Haddon W, Jr. Advances in the epidemiology of injuries as a basis for public policy. *Public Health Reports* 1980;95(5):411.
3. Robertson LS. *Injury Epidemiology.* New York: Oxford University Press, 1992.
4. Wilson M, Baker SP, Teret SP, Shock S, Garbarino J. *Saving Children: A Guide to Injury Prevention.* New York: Oxford University Press, 1991.
5. *Guns: A Public Health Approach: Making Changes in Making Guns.* May 23, 1995; Washington, D.C.: Association of Trial Lawyers of America and The Johns Hopkins Center for Gun Policy and Research, 1995.

CHAPTER I. THE SCOPE OF THE PROBLEM

1. Centers for Disease Control and Prevention, National Center for Health Statistics. Annual Summary of Births, Marriages, Divorces, and Deaths: United States, 1994. *Monthly Vital Statistics Report* 1995;43(13).
2. Annest JL, Mercy JA, Gibson DR, Ryan GW. National estimates of nonfatal firearm-related injuries: beyond the tip of the iceberg. *JAMA* 1995;273(22): 1749–1754.
3. Max W, Rice D. Shooting in the dark: estimating the cost of firearms injuries. *Health Affairs (Millwood)* 1993;171.
4. Centers for Disease Control. Mortality Database. 1995.
5. World Health Organization. *World Health Statistics.* Geneva: 1993.
6. Uniform Crime Reporting Program. *Murder and Nonnegligent Manslaughter.* U.S. Department of Justice, Federal Bureau of Investigation, 1995.
7. Centers for Disease Control. Homicide among 15–19 year old males; United States, 1963–1991. *Morbidity and Mortality Weekly Report (MMWR)* 1994;43:725–727.
8. Hargarten SW, Karlson TA, O'Brien M, Hancock J, Quebbeman EJ. Characteristics of firearms involved in fatalities. *JAMA* 1995;275(1):42.
9. Wintemute GJ, Teret SP, Kraus JF, Wright MW. The choice of weapons in firearm suicides. *American Journal of Public Health* 1988;78:824–826.
10. Card JJ. Lethality of suicidal methods and suicide risk: two distinct concepts. *Omega Journal of Death and Dying* 1974;5:37–45.
11. Centers for Disease Control. Suicide among children, adolescents, and young adults—United States 1980–1992. *MMWR* 1995;44(15):289–291.
12. Brent D, Perper J, Allman C, Moritz G, Wartella M, Zelenak J. The presence and accessibility of firearms in the homes of adolescent suicides. *JAMA* 1991;266(21):2989.
13. Kellermann AL, Rivara FP, Somes G, et al. Suicide in the home in relation to gun ownership. *New England Journal of Medicine (N Engl J Med)* 1992;327:467–472.
14. Robertson LS. *Injury Epidemiology.* New York: Oxford University Press, 1992.
15. Baker SP, O'Neill B, Ginsburg M, Li, G. *The Injury Fact Book.* New York: Oxford University Press, 1992.

16. *Guns: A Public Health Approach: Making Changes in Making Guns.* May 23, 1995; Washington, D.C.: Association of Trial Lawyers of America and The Johns Hopkins Center for Gun Policy and Research, 1995.

17. Centers for Disease Control. Deaths resulting from firearm and motor vehicle related injuries; United States, 1968–1991. *MMWR* 1994;43:37–42.

18. Kizer KW, Vassar MJ, Harry RL, Layton KD. Hospitalization charges, costs, and income for firearm-related injuries at a university trauma center. *JAMA* 1995;273:1768–1773.

19. Lalli F. The cost of one bullet: $2 million. *Money* 1994;23:7–8.

20. Martin MJ, Hunt TK, Hulley SB. The cost of hospitalization for firearm injuries. *JAMA* 1988;260:3048–3050.

21. Wintemute GJ, Wright MA. Initial and subsequent hospital costs of firearm injuries. *Journal of Trauma (J Trauma)* 1992;33:556–560.

22. Centers for Disease Control. Firearm-related years of potential life lost before age 65 years—United States, 1980–1991. *MMWR* 1994;43(33):609–616.

23. Karlson TA. Injury control and public policy. *Critical Reviews in Environmental Control (Rev Environ)* 1992;22(3/4):195–241.

24. Stover SL, DeLisa JA, Whiteneck GG. *Spinal Cord Injury: Clinical Outcomes for Model Systems.* Aspen, Co.: Aspen Publications, 1995.

CHAPTER 2. GUNS AND AMMUNITION

Primary technical references for chapters 2 and 3 include our technical reviewers and the following sources:

Diagram Group. *Weapons: An International Encyclopedia from 5000 B.C. to 2000 A.D.* New York: St. Martins Press, 1990.

Sellier KG, Kneubuehl BP. *Wound Ballistics and the Scientific Background.* Amsterdam: Elsevier, 1994.

Rees CF. *Beginner's Guide to Guns and Shooting.* U.S.A.: DBI Books, Inc., 1988.

DiMaio VJ. *Gunshot Wounds: Practical Aspects of Firearms, Ballistics, and Forensic Techniques.* Baton Rouge, Ga.: CRC Press, 1993.

Specific Sources:

1. Diagram Group. *Weapons: An International Encyclopedia from 5000 B.C. to 2000 A.D.* New York: St. Martins Press, 1990.

2. Sellier KG, Kneubuehl BP. *Wound Ballistics and the Scientific Background.* Amsterdam: Elsevier, 1994.

3. Wintemute GJ. *Ring of Fire: The Handgun Makers of Southern California.* Sacramento, Ca: Violence Prevention Research Program, 1994.

4. Wintemute GJ. The relationship between firearm design and firearm violence: handguns in the 1990s. *JAMA* 1996;275:1749–1753.

5. Teret SP, Wintemute G, Beilenson P. The firearm fatality reporting system: a proposal. *JAMA* 1992;267(22):3073.

6. Teret SP. The firearm injury reporting system revisited. *JAMA* 1996;275:70.

Sources

7. Robertson LS. *Injury Epidemiology.* New York: Oxford University Press, 1992.

CHAPTER 3. MODERN FIREARMS

1. Larson E. Wild west legacy: Ruger gun often fires if dropped, but firm sees no need for recall. *Wall Street Journal* 1993 June 24:(A);1.
2. Guns: A Public Health Approach: Making Changes in Making Guns. May 23, 1995; Washington, D.C.: Association of Trial Lawyers of America and The Johns Hopkins Center for Gun Policy and Research, 1995.
3. Chrysler Minivans: A deadly problem, but no recall. *Consumer Reports* 1995 June:378–379.
4. DiMaio VJ. *Gunshot Wounds: Practical Aspects of Firearms, Ballistics, and Forensic Techniques.* Baton Rouge: CRC Press, 1993.
5. Warner K. *Gun Digest.* U.S.A.: DBI Books, Inc., 1996.
6. Teret SP, Alexander GR, Bailey LA. The passage of Maryland's gun law: data and advocacy for injury prevention. *Journal of Public Health Policy (J Public Health Pol)* 1990;11:26–38.
7. Teret SP, Wintemute G, Beilenson P. The firearm fatality reporting system: A proposal. *JAMA* 1992;267(22):3073.
8. Teret SP. The firearm injury reporting system revisited. *JAMA* 1996;275:70.
9. Hargarten SW, Karlson TA, O'Brien M, Hancock J, Quebbeman E. Characteristics of firearms involved in fatalities. *JAMA* 1995;275(1):42.
10. Wintemute GJ. The relationship between firearm design and firearm violence: Handguns in the 1990s. *JAMA* 1996;275:1749–1753.
11. Webster DW, Chaulk CP, Teret SP. Reducing firearm injuries. *Issues in Science and Technology* 1991;7:73–79.
12. Hartman R. What assault ban? *CBS–TV: 60 Minutes.* 5 February 1995.
13. Wintemute GJ. *Ring of Fire: The Handgun Makers of Southern California.* Sacramento, Ca.: Violence Prevention Research Program, 1994.

CHAPTER 4. COMPARING FIREARMS

1. Webster DW, Champion HR, Gainer PS, Sykes L. Epidemiologic changes in gunshot wounds in Washington, D.C. *Archives of Surgery (Archiv Surgery)* 1992;127:694–698.
2. Hartman R. What assault ban? *CBS–TV: 60 Minutes.* 5 February 1995.
3. Wintemute GJ. *Ring of Fire: The Handgun Makers of Southern California.* Sacramento, Ca.: Violence Prevention Research Program, 1994.
4. Cook P. The "Saturday Night Special": an assessment of alternative definitions from a policy perspective. *The Journal of Criminal Law & Criminology (Crim Law)* 1981;72(4):1735–1745.
5. McDowall D, Loftin C, Wiersema B. Easing concealed firearms laws: effects on homicide in three states. *Crim Law* 1995;86:193–206.
6. Guns: A Public Health Approach: Making Changes in Making Guns. May 23, 1995; Washington, D.C.: Association of Trial Lawyers of America and The Johns Hopkins Center for Gun Policy and Research, 1995.

Sources

7. Wintemute GJ. The relationship between firearm design and firearm violence: handguns in the 1990s. *JAMA* 1996;275:1749–1753.

8. Barach E, Tomlanovich, M, Nowak R. Ballistics: A pathophysiologic examination of the wounding mechanisms of firearms: Part II. *J Trauma* 1986;26(4):374–383.

9. Naureckas SM, Galanter C, Naureckas ET, et al. Children's and women's ability to fire handguns. *Arch. of Pediatric and Adolescent Medicine* 1995;149:1318–1322.

10. Wintemute GJ. Firearms as a cause of death in the United States. *J Trauma* 1987;27:532–536.

11. Technology Assessment Program. *Body Armor User Guide.* Washington, D.C.: U.S. Department of Justice: National Institute of Justice: Technology Assessment Program.

12. Wintemute GJ. Homicides, handguns, and the crime gun hypothesis: Firearms used in fatal shootings of law enforcement officers, 1980 to 1989. *American Journal of Public Health* 1994;84(4):561–564.

13. Sugarmann J, Rand K. *Cease Fire: A Comprehensive Strategy to Reduce Firearms Violence.* U.S.A.: Violence Policy Center, Straight Arrow Publishers, 1994.

14. Sellier KG, Kneubuehl BP. *Wound Ballistics and the Scientific Background.* Amsterdam: Elsevier, 1994.

CHAPTER 5. INJURIES FROM FIREARMS

1. Baker SP. Injury science comes of age. *JAMA* 1989;262(16):2284.

2. Robertson LS. *Injury Epidemiology.* New York: Oxford University Press, 1992.

3. Setting the national agenda for injury control in the 1990s. In: *Position Papers from The Third National Injury Control Conference.* 22 April 1991; Denver, Co. Dept. of Health and Human Services, Public Health Service, Centers for Disease Control, 1992.

4. Sellier KG, Kneubuehl BP. *Wound Ballistics and the Scientific Background.* Amsterdam: Elsevier, 1994.

5. Unpublished Data. Hargarten SP, O'Brien M. Firearm Injury Reporting System, Medical College of Wisconsin.

6. Fackler ML, Malinowski BS. The wound profile: a visual method for quantifying gunshot wound components. *J Trauma* 1985;25.

7. Webster DW, Champion HR, Gainer PS, Sykes L. Epidemiologic changes in gunshot wounds in Washington, D.C. *Arch Surg* 1992;127:694–698.

8. McGonigal MD, Cole J, Schwab CW, Kauder DR, Rotondo MF, Angood PB. Urban firearm deaths: a five-year perspective. *J Trauma* 1993;35:532.

9. Wintemute GJ. The relationship between firearm design and firearm violence: handguns in the 1990s. *JAMA* 1996;275:1749–1753.

10. Quebbeman EJ, Hargarten S. The black talon: a new risk for percutaneous injury. *J Trauma* 1993;35:489.

11. Hargarten SW, Karlson TA, O'Brien M, Hancock J, Quebbeman E. Characteristics of firearms involved in fatalities. *JAMA* 1995;275(1):42.

Sources

12. Kellermann AL, Lee RK, Mercy JA, Banton J. The epidemiologic basis for
the prevention of firearm injuries. *Annual Review of Public Health (A R Public Health)* 1991;12:17–40.

CHAPTER 6. WHERE GUNS COME FROM

1. Sugarmann J, Rand K. *Cease Fire: A Comprehensive Strategy to Reduce Firearms Violence.* U.S.A.: Violence Policy Center, Straight Arrow Publishers, 1994.
2. Bureau of Alcohol, Tobacco, and Firearms. *Annual Firearms Manufacturing and Exportation Report.* Department of the Treasury, Bureau of Alcohol, Tobacco, and Firearms, 1946–1994.
3. Wintemute GJ. Firearms as a cause of death in the United States. *J Trauma* 1987;27:532–536.
4. *Female Persuasion: A Study of How the Firearms Industry Markets to Women and the Reality of Women and Guns.* Washington, D.C.: Violence Policy Center, 1994.
5. Stewart J, Alexander A. *Firepower: Assault Weapons in America.* Cox Newspapers, December 1987.
6. Wintemute GJ. *Advertising Firearms as Protection.* Sacramento, Ca.: Violence Prevention Research Program, June 1995.
7. Kellermann AL, Rivara FP, et al. Gun ownership as a risk factor for homicide in the home. *N Engl J Med* 1993;329(15):1084–1091.
8. Kellermann AL, Rivara FP, Somes G, et al. Suicide in the home in relation to gun ownership. *N Engl J Med* 1992;327:467–472.
9. Wintemute GJ, Teret SP, Kraus JF, Wright MA, Bradfield G. When children shoot children. *JAMA* 1987;257:3107–9.
10. Bluestein L. AAP opposes deceptive handgun ads. *American Academy of Pediatrics News* 1996 April;4–5.
11. Wintemute GJ. *Ring of Fire: The Handgun Makers of Southern California.* Sacramento, Ca.: Violence Prevention Research Program, 1994.
12. Freedman A. Fire Power. *Wall Street Journal* 1992 February 28:1
13. Hargarten SW, Karlson TA, O'Brien M, Hancock J, Quebberman E. Characteristics of firearms involved in fatalities. *JAMA* 1995;275(1):42
14. Wintemute GJ. The relationship between firearm design and firearm violence: handguns in the 1990s. *JAMA* 1996;275:1749–1753.
15. *Guns: A Public Health Approach: Making Changes in Making Guns.* May 23, 1995; Washington, D.C.: Association of Trial Lawyers of America and The Johns Hopkins Center for Gun Policy and Research, 1995.
16. Johnston D. Advocates of gun control fear results of a trade agreement with Russia. *New York Times* 1996 February 2; Sect. D:19.
17. Webster DW, Champion HR, Gainer PS, Sykes L. Epidemiologic changes in gunshot wounds in Washington, D.C. *Arch Surg* 1992;127:694–698.
18. McGonigal MD, Cole J, Schwab CW, Kauder DR, Rotondo MF, Angood PB. Urban firearm deaths: a five-year perspective. *J Trauma* 1993;35:532.

19. Stone JL, Lichtor T, Fitzgerald LF, Barrett JA, Reyes HM. Demographics of civilian cranial gunshot wounds: devastation related to escalating semiautomatic usage. *J Trauma* 1995;38:851–854.
20. Children's Safety Network. In: *Gun Dealers, USA*. National Center for Education in Maternal and Child Health, 1994.
21. Bureau of Alcohol, Tobacco, and Firearms. *Internal Monthly Report of Licensed Firearm Dealers*. Department of the Treasury, Bureau of Alcohol, Tobacco and Firearms, January–December 1995
22. Firearms and Explosives Division. *Operation Snapshot*. Bureau of Alcohol, Tobacco, and Firearms, Office of Compliance Operations, Firearms and Explosives Division, July 1993.
23. Hinds MD. A gun dealer's story: good intentions go astray. *New York Times* 1994 June 6;Sect. A:13.
24. Cook PJ, Molliconi S, Cole TB. Regulating gun markets. *Crim Law* 1995;86:59–92.
25. Cook PJ. Strategic thinking about gun markets and violence. *JAMA* 1996;275:1765–1767.
26. Wright JD, Rossi PH. *The Armed Criminal in America*. Washington, D.C.: U.S. Department of Justice, National Institute of Justice, July 1985.
27. Rand MR. *Guns and Crime: Handgun Victimization, Firearm Self-defense, and Firearm Theft*. Washington, D.C.: U.S. Department of Justice, Bureau of Justice Statistics, 1994.
28. Callahan CM, Rivara FP. Urban high school youth and handguns: a school based survey. *JAMA* 1992;267:3038–3042.
29. Sheley JF, Wright, JD *Gun Acquisition and Possession in Selected Juvenile Samples*. Washington, D.C.: National Institute of Justice, Office of Juvenile Justice and Delinquency Prevention, December 1993.
30. Baker SP. Who bought the cars in which people are injured? *Am J Public Health* 1979;69:76–78.
31. Baker SP, O'Neill B, Ginsburg M, Li G. *The Injury Fact Book*. New York: Oxford University Press, 1992.
32. Chatterjee BF, Imm P. Firearms prevalence and storage practices in Wisconsin households. *Wisconsin Medical Journal* 1996;95:286–291.
33. Weil DS, Hemenway D. Loaded guns in the home: analysis of a national random survey of gun owners. *JAMA* 1992;267:3033–3037.
34. Brent D, Perper J, Allman C, Moritz G, Wartella M, Zelenak J. The presence and accessibility of firearms in the homes of adolescent suicides. *JAMA* 1991;266(21):2989.
35. Kleck G. Crime control through the private use of armed force. *Social Problems* 1988;35:11.

CHAPTER 7. HOW GUNS ARE CURRENTLY REGULATED

1. Christoffel T, Teret SP. *Protecting the Public: Legal Issues in Injury Prevention*. New York: Oxford University Press, 1993.

2. Vernick JS, Teret SP. Firearms and health: The right to be armed with accurate information about the second amendment. *Am J Public Health* 1993;83:1773–1777.

3. Sugarmann J, Rand K. *Cease Fire: A Comprehensive Strategy to Reduce Firearms Violence*. U.S.A: Violence Policy Center, Straight Arrow Publishers, 1994.

4. Hartman R. What assault ban? *CBS–TV: 60 Minutes*. February 5 1995.

5. Bergman AB, ed. *Political Approaches to Injury Control at the State Level*. Seattle, Wa.: University of Washington Press, 1992:vii.

6. Teret SP, Alexander GR, Bailey LA. The passage of Maryland's gun law: data and advocacy for injury prevention. *J Public Health Policy* 1990;11:26–38.

7. Loftin C, McDowall D, Wiersema B, Cottoy TJ. Effects of restrictive licensing on homicide and suicide in the District of Columbia. *N Engl J Med* 1991;325:1615.

8. Weil DS, Knox RC. Effects of limiting handgun purchases on interstate transfer of firearms. *JAMA* 1996;275:1759–1761.

9. Friedman AM. Carrying concealed weapons may increase homicide rates. *HELP Network News* 1995:1.

10. Verhovek SH. In Texas, the "inner child" has finger on the trigger. *New York Times* 1995 November 8;Sect. A:1

11. Karlson TA. Injury control and public policy. *Rev Environ* 1992;22 (3/4):195–241.

12. Teret SP, DeFrancesco S, Bailey S. Gun deaths and home rule: a case of local regulation of a local public health problem. *American Journal of Preventive Medicine* 1993;9(3):44–46.

13. Vernick J. Preemption of local gun laws: Questions and answers. *HELP Network News* 1995.

14. Pommer M. Senate joins in scrapping city gun laws. *Capital Times* 1995 November 10; Sect. A:1

15. Smothers R. A tax debate focuses on destruction science. *New York Times* 1993 November 7;Sect. A:22.

16. Wintemute GJ. *Ring of Fire: The Handgun Makers of Southern California*. Sacramento, Ca.: Violence Prevention Research Program, 1994.

CHAPTER 8. STRATEGIES FOR REDUCING DEATHS AND INJURIES

1. Karlson TA. Injury control and public policy. *Rev Environ* 1992;22(3/4): 195–241.

2. Baker SP. Without guns, do people kill people? *Am J Public Health* 1985;75(6):587.

3. Christoffel T, Teret SP. *Protecting the Public: Legal Issues in Injury Prevention*. New York: Oxford University Press, 1993.

4. *Guns: A Public Health Approach: Making Changes in Making Guns*. May 23, 1995; Washington, D.C.: Association of Trial Lawyers of America and The Johns Hopkins Center for Gun Policy and Research, 1995.

5. *Firearms Litigation Reporter* 1995;9(1).

6. Robinson G. Legal help. *HELP Network News* 1995:4.

Sources

7. Wintemute GJ, Teret SP, Kraus JF, Wright MA, Bradfield G. When children shoot children. *JAMA* 1987;257:3107–3109.

8. *Accidental Shootings.* United States, General Accounting Office, March 1991.

9. Friedman AM. Carrying concealed weapons may increase homicide rates. *Help Network News* 1995:1.

10. Hargarten SW, Karlson TA, O'Brien M, Hancock J, Quebbeman E. Characteristics of firearms involved in fatalities. *JAMA* 1995;275(1):42.

11. Wintemute GJ. *Ring of Fire: The Handgun Makers of Southern California.* Sacramento, Ca.: Violence Prevention Research Program, 1994.

12. Freedman A. Fire power. *Wall Street Journal* 1992 February 28.

13. *Firearms Litigation Reporter.* 1994–1995;8.

14. Hartman R. What assault ban? *CBS–TV: 60 Minutes.* 1995 February 5.

15. Wintemute GJ. The relationship between firearm design and firearm violence: handguns in the 1990s. *JAMA* 1996;275:1749–1753.

16. Barach E, Tomlanovich M, Nowak R. Ballistics: A pathophysiologic examination of the wounding mechanisms of firearms: Part II. *J Trauma* 1986;26(4):374–383.

17. Sugarmann J, Rand K. *Cease Fire: A Comprehensive Strategy to Reduce Firearms Violence.* U.S.A.: Violence Policy Center, Straight Arrow Publishers, 1994.

18. Sellier KG, Kneubuehl BP. *Wound Ballistics and the Scientific Background.* Amsterdam: Elsevier, 1994.

19. Loftin C, McDowall D, Wiersema B, Cottoy TJ. Effects of restrictive licensing on homicide and suicide in the District of Columbia. *N Engl J Med* 1991;325:1615.

20. Hinds MD. A gun dealer's story: good intentions go astray. *New York Times* 1994 June 6;Sect. A:13.

21 Cook PJ, Molliconi S, Cole TB. Regulating gun markets. *Crim Law* 1995;86:59–92.

22. Cook PJ. Strategic thinking about gun markets and violence. *JAMA* 1996; 275:1765–1767.

23. Federal program will track sales of guns to youths. *New York Times* 1996 July 8;Sect. A:1

24. Teret SP, Wintemute G, Beilenson P. The firearm fatality reporting system: a proposal. *JAMA* 1992;267(22):3073.

25. Teret SP. The firearm injury reporting system revisited. *JAMA* 1996;275:70.

26. Kellermann AL, Lee RK, Mercy JA, Banton J. The epidemiologic basis for the prevention of firearm injuries. *Ann Rev Public Health* 1991;12:17–40.

27. Kellermann AL. Firearm-related violence—what we don't know is killing us. *Am J Public Health* 1994;84:541–542.

28. Kellermann AL. Obstacles to firearm and violence research. *Health Affairs (Millwood)* 1993;12:142–153.

29. Herbert, Bob. More NRA mischief. *New York Times* 1996 July 5;Sect. A:11.

30. Jagger J, Dietz P. Death and injury by firearms: Who cares? *JAMA* 1988; 255:3143.

Sources

INDEX

Index

About the Authors

One of the first people to earn a PH.D. in injury epidemiology, Trudy A. Karlson researches and writes about injuries and their preventions. Over the past twenty years, she has worked on the prevention of injuries from truck, car, and motorcycle crashes, farm tractors, dog bites, motor boat propellers, and guns. She is a senior scientist at the University of Wisconsin-Madison in the Center for Health Systems Research and Analysis.

Dr. Stephen W. Hargarten, M.D., M.P.H. is an associate professor in the Department of Emergency Medicine at the Medical College of Wisconsin. He has a long-standing interest in injury prevention policy and research.